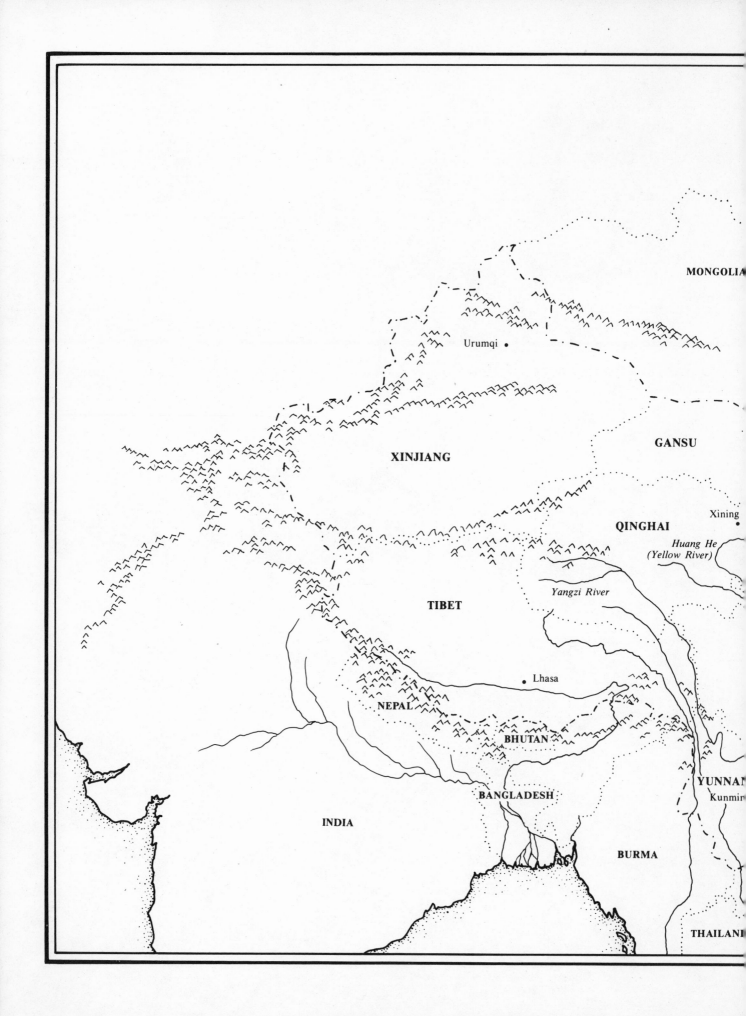

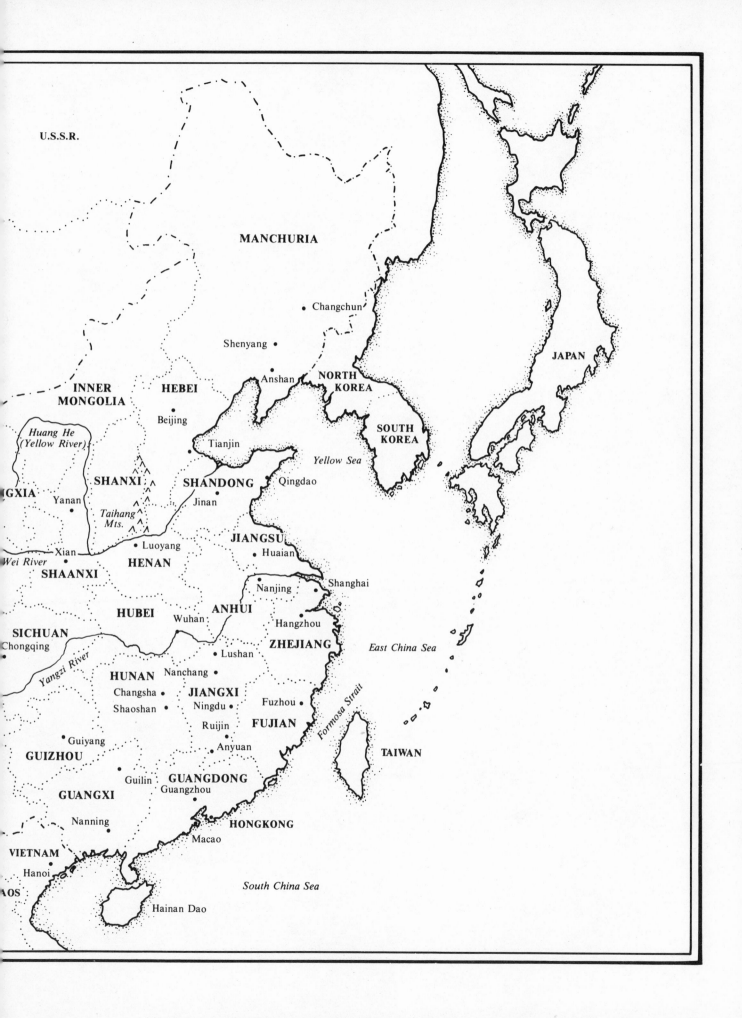

To Embrace the Moon

To Embrace the Moon

An Illustrated Biography of

Mao Zedong

by Ed Hammond

LANCASTER-MILLER PUBLISHERS/ASIAN HUMANITIES PRESS
Berkeley, California   1980

Book designed by Carol Egenolf, cover based on a design by
Myland McRevey, maps by Jane Bernard, production by Gail
Tsukiyama, Edward Aréna and George Kelly.

Cloth: ISBN 0-89581-454-4
Paper: ISBN 0-89581-502-8

Library of Congress Cataloging in Publication Data

Hammond, Ed, 1945-
    To Embrace the Moon.

    Bibliography: p.
    1. Mao, Tse-tung, 1893-1976. 2. Heads of
state—China—Biography. I. Title.
DS778.M3H34   951.05' 092'4 [B] 80-21329
ISBN O-89581-454-4
ISBN O-89581-502-8 (pbk.)

To Steve, who helped

A NOTE ON PRONUNCIATION

This book uses the international system adopted in 1979 for transcribing Chinese characters. The only exceptions are for Chiang Kaishek and Sun Yatsen, two well-known figures whose names historically have been pronounced in southern Chinese dialects and as such are not susceptible to standardized transcription.

The following is the Pinyin system's alphabet with American English equivalents.

a as in *far*
ao as in *cow*
b as in *be*
c as in *its*
ch as in *church*
d as in *do*
e as in *her*
f as in *foot*
g as in *go*
h as in *her*
i as in *eat* (except when preceded by c, ch, r, s, sh, z, or zh, then as in *sir*)
j as in *jeep*
k as in *kind*
l as in *land*
m as in *me*
n as in *no*
o as in *law*
ou as in *owe*
p as in *par*
q as in *chin*
r as in *right*
s as in *sister*
sh as in *shore*
t as in *top*
u as in *too*
w as in *want*
x as in *she*
y as in *yet*
z as in *zero*
zh as in *jump*

Contents

JINGGANSHAN REVISITED

Storms pounded,
Flags waved,
Before the realm was settled.

Now 38 years have gone by
In the twinkling of an eye
And we can mount the nine heavens to embrace the moon
Or we can descend the five seas to catch a turtle.

The talking, laughing, and triumphant songs come back.
Nothing in this world is difficult.
Only you must be willing to climb.

Mao Zedong 1965
Written after a visit to the scene of the start of his guerilla career.

1893-1921

MAO'S HOME IN SHAOSHAN. HIS FAMILY LIVED ON THE LEFT, TILED SIDE OF THE BUILDING.

OPEN REBELLION

By a lotus pond in a remote village in central China, an event occurred in the early years of this century that may have changed the course of history irrevocably. A boy, barely a teenager, confronted his father. The boy, tall and round-cheeked, was no match physically for the gaunt-faced man hardened by years of military service. Yet in willpower they met like the proverbial irresistible force and immovable object. The father demanded a full apology from the boy, who had just cursed him in front of guests. The son refused. Indeed, he felt he deserved some expression of regret from the man who had derided him and called him lazy in front of others, thus provoking an imprecation in heated defense. Now, verbally locking horns outside the house, they reached an impasse, with the boy threatening to jump in the pond and drown.

Eventually the father relented. He had demanded the ritual *kowtow,* the elaborate kneeling and prostration performed to show subservience to the emperor and high officials. The boy agreed to a partial kowtow, on only one knee, if the father agreed not to beat him afterward. The man assented. Face was saved. The incident ended.

"I learned that when I defended my rights by open rebellion my father relented, but when I remained weak and submissive he only cursed and beat me the more." Such was the lesson taught to the young Mao Zedong by this incident. He went on from there to become the foremost rebel and revolutionary of the twentieth century, if not of all time.

The small village of Shaoshan, nestled in the hills of China's south-central Hunan province, offered an unlikely environment for the nurturing of a modern leader. Lying 150 miles south of the Yangzi river and 600 miles southwest of Shanghai, Shaoshan remained isolated from China's vigorous internal commerce and the influence of foreign trade. Electricity for lighting was unknown there until 1966. When Mao was born on December 26, 1893, the area preserved the millennia-old habits of Chinese peasants and Confucian culture.

Perhaps Shaoshan's hills offer some explanation. The highest rises only 1,700 feet, and has a Buddhist temple on top. Mao made the ascent at a very early age, accompanying his devout mother.

Legend holds that one of China's first emperors climbed these hills and, enchanted by their beauty, devised a musical form peculiar to the region. Significantly, the legend maintains that Shaoshan became the birthplace of phoenixes and "great men doing great deeds." Apart from this mythology, Shaoshan's hills must have conveyed another message to Mao, one that he preserved in a poem: Nothing in this world is impossible/ Only you must be willing to climb.

Whatever the cause, the inhabitants of the area all share an indomitable, rebellious spirit. Mao's father was no exception. Born to a poor peasant who worked a half-acre of land, Mao Renshen was forced to leave the village at age sixteen, when his father had to sell the family plot to a landlord. For seven long years Mao Renshen served in the army, saving his pay and living frugally, waiting for the day he could return to the village and reclaim the land. When he did get back, he had enough to buy the land and get married to an older woman, as was the custom, from a village sixteen miles away. They soon had a boy, Mao Zedong, and then another, Mao Zemin, three years later.

Mao Zedong thus was born into a poor peasant family. But it did not stay poor. Mao Renshen drove himself and his family. Young Mao was sent to work in the fields when he was six. Gradually more land was bought. Money was made. Investments brought further gains and the embryo of a rice-shipping business, for the land produced more rice than the family could eat, and Mao Renshen had to sell the surplus. By the end of his life, Mao Renshen had been able to put a tile roof on the mud-walled house with beaten-earth floors that his father had built 40 years before.

For Mao Zedong, his father represented "the Ruling Power." Mao Renshen would reward hired help with small delicacies like eggs after a hard day's work in the field, but he made his own sons do without, in order to increase the family wealth. He sent the young Mao to the village school, but complained when he stayed up at night reading; it wasted precious lamp oil. Against such patent unfairness, he and his brother and his mother formed "the Opposition," though his mother as a good Chinese wife would never openly contradict her husband, and she advised her sons to moderate their demands.

MAO AT THE TIME OF HIS MOTHER'S DEATH. FROM THE RIGHT WE SEE MAO, HIS UNCLE, HIS FATHER, HIS BROTHER ZETAN.

FROM THE RIGHT, MAO, HIS MOTHER, HIS BROTHERS ZEMIN AND ZETAN.

Mao's political career can be seen as starting from his original rebellion against "the Ruling Power" and his disavowal of counsels of moderation within "the Opposition." The terms are his own. He used them jokingly when he told his life's story to the American journalist Edgar Snow; yet they give an insight into his character, into how he perceived himself. Moreover, it was about this same time, around 1907, that larger political issues intruded on Mao's consciousness and his small village.

In 1906 a major famine had devastated Hunan. In Changsha, the provincial capital forty miles from Shaoshan, crowds clustered and petitioned the governor for relief. None too wisely, he mocked them by taunting, "Why haven't you got food? There is plenty in the city. I always have enough." This angered the petitioners, who rioted, sacking the governor's offices and looting local granaries. A general revolt was touched off. Three provincial armies had to be called in to suppress it. When it was over, rebel heads festooned the city gates of Changsha, and many of its citizens had fled in fright.

Bean merchants escaping south brought news of all this to Shaoshan. The sheer excitement of the incident provoked endless discussion in the school. Mao claimed that the news had a particularly strong impression on him, since he realized the rebellious petitioners were "ordinary people" like his own family.

After the Changsha rebellion came a smaller one, by a secret society in Shaoshan, when a lawsuit by a local landlord was decided in his favor. The society members rejected the judgment and fled to the mountains, where troops finally hunted them down and beheaded their leader. A year later poor peasants launched another rebellion and seized rice supplies in transport, some of which were owned by Mao's father.

These local incidents fit into a pattern of revolt at the time. The traditions of more than a thousand years were collapsing. Foreign incursions, both military and cultural, had sapped the strength of the Qing dynasty. Some reforms were made to save it. In 1905 the classical examination system that had accredited government officials for a millennium was abolished in the hope that some more up-to-date civil-service system might take its

place. But revolutionaries were pressing for even more radical change, and effective government was being destroyed in the crunch. In 1908, the death of the emperor and his mother—a figure rather like Queen Victoria—left a vacuum at the center of power. Without its linchpin, the edifice of state required only a slight push to be toppled.

Mao faintly perceived these changes. A "radical" teacher at his school preached iconoclasm and railed against Buddhism. A book, *Words of Warning,* that came into Mao's hands told of the danger China was in unless it industrialized. A pamphlet foretold China's dismemberment after opening with the words, "Alas, China will be subjugated!" But at the time the ruling power that concerned him most was his father.

Mao Renshen made plans for his fourteen-year-old son to become a rice merchant. He secured an apprenticeship for him, and, in an effort to put some stability in the boy's life, arranged a marriage as well. In 1908 the teenaged Mao Zedong married a young woman several years his senior. However, the lesson of "open rebellion" carried the day. The headstrong boy refused to consummate the marriage, much to the shame of both families. Instead, he left the village to stay with a friend. When he returned, he lived at home, but still refused to bend to his father's will. He escaped into the heroic tales of the past preserved in popular classics, *The Water-Margin Chronicle* and *Romance of the Three Kingdoms.* And so conditions stayed until a cousin told him of a new school in the small town where his mother's family lived. The school was considered quite "radical" and attracted Mao with the promise of Western knowledge. Of course, Mao's father opposed his plans, but finally relented when friends assured him that Mao's "advanced" education would allow him to make more money. With his father's blessings, Mao set off on his own.

SCHOOLING

Mao was now fully grown and quite tall. But his physical growth had outpaced his advance in knowledge. He had read only a handful of books—not necessarily with much understanding—and had not really been outside his own small village.

Not surprisingly, his arrival at the new school was a shock—for both parties.

The school Mao wanted to attend turned out to be a primary school. When he arrived, the boys playing in the schoolyard were all several years younger and significantly smaller. (Mao was rather large for a Chinese.) Mao, rumpled and dirty, carrying a long pole with his clothes on one end and his two favorite books on the other, was mistaken for an ordinary worker. The school janitor would not let him pass. The well-dressed sons of merchants and landlords quickly turned from playing to jeering at the odd creature at the gate demanding admission.

Mao persisted. Having walked fifteen miles to get to the school, he would not be easily stopped. When the headmaster came out to check on the commotion, Mao again demanded to be admitted. The headmaster examined him and discovered that he had studied for only a few years in the village. Mao was nearly denied admission. But another teacher, impressed by Mao' fervor, intervened. Mao was given a temporary admission, on condition that he take extra lessons to catch up.

The determined Mao, just over sixteen years old, needed no further incentive. For the next year he devoured every book that came into his sight. The boy from the small village knew he had a lot of work to make up.

Exposed directly for the first time to the writings of Kang Youwei and Liang Qichao, famous reformists who advocated a constitutional monarchy for China, Mao was easily converted to their political philosophy. Mao was also impressed by another book that he found, *Great Heroes of the World*. After reading of their exploits, he developed a great admiration for Washington, Lincoln, Napoleon, and others. A quarter of a century later he would still recite the line, ''After eight years of difficult war, Washington won victory and built up his nation.''

Absorbing this material quickly, Mao was soon ready to move on. In the spring of 1911, he applied for admission to a more advanced middle school in Changsha. To his surprise and great pleasure, he was accepted. The village boy moved to the big city that fall.

Mao barely had time to settle in before the 1911 revolution broke out. It had been brewing for a long time. Kang and Liang, the reformists whom Mao had discovered and ''worshiped'' in the primary school the year before, had in fact been most influential politically more than a decade earlier. After the turn of the century, they had been supplanted by the group around Dr. Sun Yatsen, who advocated the elimination of the Manchus and the establishment of a republic. In Hunan province itself these revolutionaries had instigated several revolts, and had had a hand in the riots Mao heard about in his small village.

Much of this was news to Mao. After all, he had never read a newspaper before he arrived in Changsha, and did not even know the emperor had died until he left his village. But once he was exposed to the revolutionaries' propaganda, he immediately joined in. Swelling with enthusiasm, he wrote his own revolutionary manifesto and posted it on the school wall, in much the same way that the Red Guards would do in the Cultural Revolution.

When revolutionary troops seized power in Wuhan, two hundred miles to the north, Mao decided to go there. But on the day that he set out, the revolution came to Changsha. Mao, outside the city, could only watch from a distance as revolutionary forces took over. Now Mao did not have to go to Wuhan; he stayed in Changsha and joined the revolutionary army.

The next six months proved to be an unnecessary but valuable hiatus in Mao's schooling. It was unnecessary because the revolutionary army was never used. The Manchus were completely corrupt and incapable of self-defense. Dynastic rule dissolved virtually overnight. Yet the experience was valuable, because in the army Mao associated with common soldiers and workers, and had the time to read newspapers, which gave him his first exposure to the concept of socialism. But nothing much came from this at the time. Mao simply returned to civilian life when he realized the army would not be used.

Mao did not return to the middle school; instead, he began a search for a ''career.'' He studied advertisements in the newspapers and consulted with friends, looking for a school that would prepare him for a profession in which he could serve the revolution. The search had many strange twists and turns. At first a police school seemed promis-

THE REVOLUTIONARY GOVERNMENT OF 1911. SUN YATSEN IS IN THE FRONT ROW, FIFTH FROM THE LEFT.

A SHOT OF THE TROOPS THAT STARTED THE 1911 REVOLUTION.

ing. Mao registered to enter, but before he could start, an ad for a soap-making school led him to change his mind. He thought that by studying soap-making he could serve the country and make some money. He changed his mind again when a friend recommended law school. Finally another friend's recommendation persuaded him to try a business school.

After many false starts and lost registration fees, Mao entered the business school—with his father's approval, of course. He left in disgust after a month. All the classes were conducted in English; yet the school offered no course to learn English.

Mao returned to middle school, but lasted only six months. The program did not satisfy his intellectual needs. He turned next to the provincial library, where for six months he sustained his body with two meager rice cakes a day while he slaked his intellectual thirst by reading about the world. For the first time he saw a map of all the continents and seas. And he read, in translation, leading Western thinkers like Darwin, Rousseau, and Montesquieu. His private studies might have continued indefinitely had his parents not intervened and demanded that he enroll in a regular school.

His parents demands were made more imperative by another problem. He could no longer live cheaply at the guild house which his district made available for its own residents while they were in the capital. The other lodgers were mostly students and soldiers, and the two groups had become intensely hostile to one another. One night the soldiers decided to attack the students. Mao escaped by fleeing and hiding in the toilet room. Fearing for his safety, he decided he had to move out, and therefore had to find some sort of regular school with student dormitories.

He settled on what was to become the First Hunan Normal School, a teachers' college. The selection process was, as usual, rather haphazard. Two friends recommended the place because they wanted to go there and have Mao accompany them. Mao wrote the essays that got all three admitted, allowing Mao to joke later that the school admitted him three times. Nevertheless, the choice was ideal. The school had no tuition, and room and board was cheap. And the education that Mao thought would make him a schoolteacher in fact prepared him to become a professional revolutionary.

The effects of this education might have been predicted by a glance at the faculty. Yang Changji, the ethics professor, ardently advocated the New Culture movement, which had just begun in Beijing. Mao became one of his most devoted students, and would later marry his daughter. Xu Teli, another teacher, exemplified iconoclasm. Unlike the other teachers who rode to school in rickshas or sedan chairs, Xu, true to his poor peasant background, ostentatiously walked. A promoter of vigorous exercise and vegetarianism, he best displayed his intensity in 1910, when he sliced his finger to sign a revolutionary petition in blood. Mao helped Xu run a literacy class for workers. Finally, "Big Beard" Yuan, a man more concerned with prose than politics, forced Mao to master a difficult classical essay style. Mao's later strength as a political leader depended in part on the writing ability that he first learned from Yuan.

Then there was the student body. Cai Hesen, who became Mao's best friend, was an ardent patriot and New Culturist. His equally fiery sister, Cai Zhang, enrolled at a nearby girl's school, had run away from home when she was ten to escape an arranged marriage. He Shuheng, another student, joined with Mao in organizing the New People's Study Society, a precursor of the Communist party. Two brothers named Xiao also shared Mao's enthusiasms, and one Xiao Yu, later accompanied Mao on a summer-long journey through the hills and valleys of Hunan province. This band of young revolutionaries all pursued political careers, and all became important figures in the Communist party (except for Xiao Yu, who was influential in the Nationalist party).

From 1913 to 1918, the years Mao attended the Hunan Normal School, the progressive students gave serious thought only to the national future. They could not be bothered by flirtation or romance—and for good reason. The nation was in trouble.

The 1911 revolution had brought to power not a strong republic, but a weak and vainglorious military dictator, Yuan Shikai, who was fair game for imperialist intrigues. In 1915 the Japanese presented him with a series of demands, the infamous "Twenty-one Demands," which gave Japan effective control over the Shandong peninsula, Manchuria, Inner Mongolia, the southeastern coast, and the Yangzi valley. In addition, they

REVOLUTIONARY TROOPS DURING ONE OF THE BRIEF PERIODS OF FIGHTING.

STUDENTS OF THE FIRST HUNAN NORMAL SCHOOL. MAO WEARS A DARK SHORT JACKET. CAI HESEN HAS A COAT WITH A FUR COLLAR.

required Japanese advisors to be employed throughout the government. If granted, these demands would have made China a virtual Japanese colony.

Protests spread like prairie fire among patriotic groups. In Changsha, Mao led street demonstrations and spoke out against "this extraordinary humiliation." As secretary of the student association, he tried to involve his school more directly, but without success. The headmaster was wary of direct political involvement, and threatened to expel Mao because of his public activities. Only support from his fellow students and teachers prevented his expulsion.

The protests were not enough to prevent Yuan from acceding to most of the demands. However, they did destroy his political authority. By year's end, a virtual civil war was launched against him and his plans to restore the monarchy. Confronted by declining political fortunes, he retired in shame and died suddenly of uremia—many said of a "broken heart"—in June 1916. At that point China made its long descent into "warlordism," a phenomenon of unbridled military power and continual civil war as different factions vied for military and political supremacy. By 1917 warlords and their troops covered the land, often looting or destroying anything that got in their way.

Warlordism gave Mao his first taste of guerrilla war. Among his responsibilities at the time was the school's self-defense forces. Mao drilled both students and teachers. Even the senior faculty obeyed his commands, no doubt because of his earlier stint in the army, but these "troops" were no match for warlord soldiers, who were used to having their own way. When some of these were billeted at the school against the administrators' wishes, it was up to Mao to drive them out. His plan was simple—and dangerous. Late at night he and the other students rushed the troops' barracks, shouting that their commander had been defeated, enemy troops had arrived, and they should surrender. In the noise and confusion, the ill-trained warlord troops panicked and fled, leaving behind their weapons. The newly armed self-defense forces never heard from them again—and Mao had scored his first military victory.

Mao also made a mark as a revolutionary prop-

agandist in 1917. In *New Youth* magazine, established two years earlier as the organ of the New Culture movement, he published an article on physical culture, complete with exercises which were probably devised to train his schoolmates in self-defense. As he argued, "If our bodies are not strong, we will be afraid as soon as we see soldiers." The main thrust of the argument, however, focused on patriotism. China is weak because its people are weak, wrote Mao, and exercise is an important step in national regeneration. Students should exercise to defend the country.

Mao practiced what he preached. Along with his friends, he wandered through the countryside braving the elements. On days when the sun beat down, they shed their shirts to take "sun baths," and when it rained they took rain baths. In November they leaped into icy streams. During that summer, in 1917, Mao and Xiao Yu wandered about Hunan penniless, experiencing the lives of beggars as they inquired into the social conditions of peasants and workers.

In the spring of 1918, Mao graduated from the Hunan Normal School without any prospects of a career. His political activity with the New People's Study Society occupied much of his interest and time, but offered no paying job. Many of his closest associates were planning to go to France, where they would participate in a government-sponsored work-study program. Mao considered this, but concluded that he did not know enough about his own country and could more profitably spend his time in China. Nevertheless, he did decide to accompany them as far as Beijing while they prepared for their departure. This choice had a major impact on Mao's life.

BEIJING

By 1918 Beijing University had become an intellectual mecca for China's patriotic youth. Its reorganization several years earlier had brought in China's leading thinkers, making the school the home for debates on the direction of China's future. Westernization, traditionalism, populism, anarchism—virtually every school of thought was represented, and usually by its leading spokesperson. Naturally, the Hunanese students headed there to prepare for their trip to France.

Mao arrived with his friends and on borrowed funds. They enrolled in the preparatory program; he immediately went in search of a job. Luck was with him. His old ethics teacher from Hunan, Yang Changji, had transferred to Beijing University the year before. Yang put Mao in touch with Li Dazhao, the university librarian, who found him a part-time job.

Mao's life in Beijing was simple but happy. During the day he worked in the library, handling minor tasks like registering the names of newspaper readers. At night he slept at "Three-Eyes Well," where the boarders were so crowded together that they had to warn one another when they wanted to turn over on the bed. During his free time Mao got to see the wonders of Beijing and witnessed the change of seasons in the parks. Ancient poems suddenly came alive as plum blossoms flowered and ice crystals made "winter-jewelled" trees. Even at work he had the opportunity to see famous intellectuals, though they seldom had time for a lowly library assistant with an uncultivated southern accent. He did better with the students in the philosophy and journalism clubs, and made several new friends there.

His six months in Beijing were also a period of uncertainty. Politically he flirted with anarchism, but also joined a Marxist study group sponsored by Li Dazhao, his boss. Emotionally he "fell in love" with Yang Kaihui, his old professor's daughter, but she was only seventeen and he was twenty-five. Moreover, his part-time job could hardly have financed a family. Finally, there was his family situation. His mother, to whom he had always been close, had died of tuberculosis just before he went to Beijing. He may have gone there partly to forget his sorrow at her loss. Certainly he wanted to get away from his father, who was complaining about his educational expenses. But Mao was unhappy at leaving behind Zemin and another, much younger brother, Zetan, both of whom were studying in Changsha. He would assume full responsibility for them less than a year later, when his father passed away from typhoid fever, but he was already teenaged Zetan's guardian in Changsha.

With his life on an uncharted course, Mao left Beijing at the same time as the original Hunanese group. They were headed for Shanghai and a boat to France. He intended to see them off, then go home to Changsha. The trip was a grand adventure. Mao left with only a ticket to nearby Tianjin. A fortunate last-minute loan allowed him to purchase a ticket for Pukou, just outside Nanjing. The train passed through Shandong province, and despite his iconoclasm Mao did not pass up the chance to climb sacred Mount Tai or visit the grave of Confucius. In Pukou he was broke again and, worse yet, a thief stole his shoes. But, in another stroke of luck, he met a Hunanese friend outside the railway station, and borrowed enough for new shoes and passage to Shanghai. Once there, he found that the work-study program had allocated funds for his return to Changsha, since he had helped organize the program; so, in April 1919, after waving goodbye to his friends at the dock, he boarded a train for Hunan.

MAY FOURTH

Back in Changsha, Mao had just secured a teaching job in a primary school when the May Fourth incident jolted the previously dormant Chinese people. Since 1915, students like Mao had been opposed to Japanese encroachments; but society in general had expected that the end of World War I would bring relief, since China had joined the Allies, and President Wilson had promised a "peace without annexations." The Treaty of Versailles dashed these hopes. Wilson, under pressure from the other Allies and his own advisors, recognized special Japanese rights in Shandong, claims based on concessions wrung from the weak Yuan Shikai and subsequent corrupt warlord governments. Chinese public opinion boiled over in response. The leading Shanghai newspaper railed, "Whoever expects help from others is doomed to be disappointed. Let our people understand today once and for all that their only course is to act by themselves."

The students took the lead. Some 5,000 of them demonstrated against the treaty in Beijing. They attacked the house of the foreign minister, and beat up the former minister to Japan, who had signed some of the concessionary pacts. Arrests by police led to a general strike which spread through China,

BEIJING STUDENTS DEMONSTRATING.

MAO IN CHANGSHA, 1919.

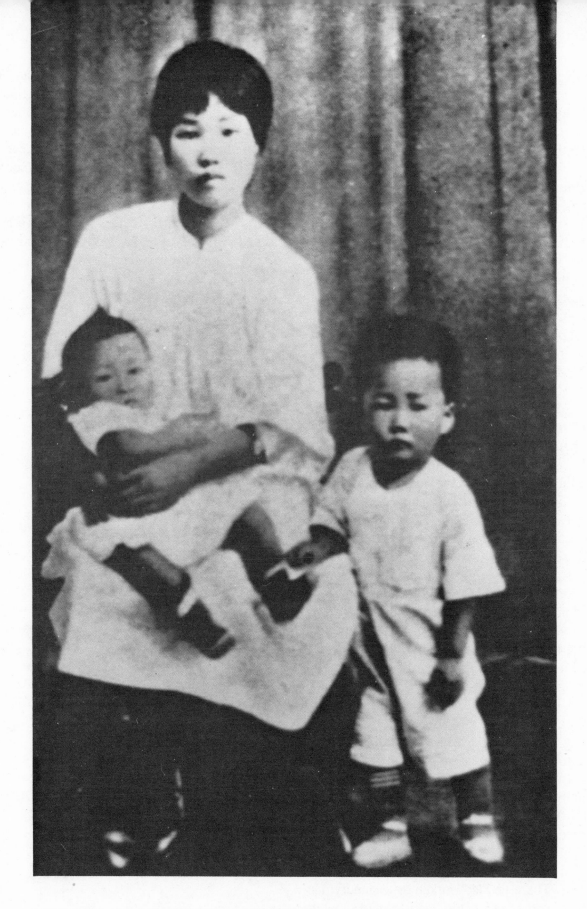

MAO'S WIFE, YANG KAIHUI, AND THEIR CHILDREN ANQING AND ANYING.

touching all segments of the populace.

In Changsha, Mao, fresh from Beijing, led the new United Students' Association, and coordinated their local activities with those of the recently emerged national student federation in pressing for a boycott of Japanese goods and support for national industries. Mao addressed the merchants of Changsha and urged them to form a committee to enforce the boycott.

At the same time, Mao also promoted more radical ideas of national regeneration. He introduced the New People's Study Society to Marxist concepts that he had leaned in Beijing from Li Dazhao. To the general public he preached a version of populism through his writings in the weekly *Xiang River Review,* which first appeared in July 1919. Mao's three-part article, "The Great Union of the Masses," served as its manifesto. Mao proposed to unite peasants, workers, students, rickshaw boys, policemen, and others to defeat "powerful people, aristocrats, and capitalists."

Mao's radicalism attracted official attention. Once the popular furor subsided, the local warlord, Zhang Jingyao, moved in to suppress the review and the student association. Mao turned to other magazines and newspapers as outlets for his ideas. There he not only denounced warlords and Japan, but also used a young woman's suicide as the occasion to inveigh against the injustice of the traditional woman's role and to demand sexual equality. But he concentrated most of his attention on overthrowing Zhang Jingyao. The effort produced a massive student strike in December, but failed to topple Zhang. In January, amid rumors that his life was in danger, Mao left Hunan.

He traveled upriver to Wuhan and then to Beijing, making money as a stringer for Changsha papers while trying to drum up support for Hunan autonomy. In Beijing he visited the Yang family, and found his former professor laid up with pneumonia. When the old man died soon after, his wife returned to Changsha and took Yang Kaihui with her. Mao could not follow his beloved. Instead he went to Shanghai, still agitating against Zhang Jingyao. There he also worked as a laundryman, washing clothes and then delivering them about the city.

That summer Zhang was finally overthrown, though by another warlord almost as bad. Mao was able to return. His alma mater, the Hunan Normal School, offered him the position of principal at an associated primary school. He gladly accepted. With this new-found financial security and social status, he rented a tiny cottage, "the Clear Water Pool House," just outside the city, and soon after married Yang Kaihui. They were to have two sons. But this marriage, though consummated, also failed to settle Mao down. Important changes, already in the works, prevented him from becoming just another provincial schoolteacher.

1921-1927

FOUNDATION OF THE CHINESE COMMUNIST PARTY

In the summer of 1921, about a dozen young Chinese met at a girls' school in Shanghai. Ensconsed on the second floor, beyond public view and Chinese control, since the school was in the French-run area of the city, they worked intently, discussing the issues confronting China.

The school janitor, who also worked as a cook and was the only regular employee around during summer vacation, noticed that the group was very strange. They spoke with dialects from all over China. This was uncommon behavior, because many dialects were completely incomprehensible to people from other parts of the country; the janitor himself could not understand some of the young men. Suspicious of what he did not comprehend, the janitor notified the police.

Plainclothes detectives began an investigation. One, perhaps by accident, walked into a meeting. He was quickly asked his business, and his reply, that he was looking for a nearby office, satisfied his interrogators. He left, only to return shortly with a dozen armed police for support. By this time all but two of the young men were gone. These two were questioned and released.

Such was the conspiratorial setting that gave birth to the Chinese Communist party. The young men in question were delegates from all over China—Beijing, Shanghai, Guangzhou, Wuhan, Jinan, Changsha—and even from Japan. They represented only about fifty other Communists scattered around the country, but, more importantly, they felt they were acting on behalf of an idea whose time had come. After the police interfered in Shanghai, they moved on to continue their work. The congress concluded in a boat on a lake south of Shanghai, with the delegates posing as vacationing gentlemen intent only on idle chatter. The delegate from Changsha, who was therefore a founder of the Communist party, was Mao Zedong.

Mao's Communist career began almost fortuitously. When he met Li Dazhao, the university librarian in Beijing, his primary interest was in a job. But Li, only five years older, apparently also aroused Mao's interest in Marxism, which Li himself had just discovered in the wake of the Russian revolution. Mao leaned more toward anarchism,

THE FIRST COMMUNIST PARTY CONGRESS FINISHED ON A BOAT SIMILAR TO THIS ONE.

AN ARTIST'S RENDITION OF THE FIRST COMMUNIST GROUP IN HUNAN.

but consented to join the study group organized by Li. Thus, ironically, in April 1919 it was an uncommitted Zedong who upon his return introduced Marxism to Hunan, specifically to his old group, the New People's Study Society.

During 1919, Marxist ideas percolated through May Fourth propaganda. Mao, for one, denounced warlord and capitalist alike. By early 1920, these ideas carried more weight, as the May Fourth activists ran aground on the shoals of intractable political realities. Organizations collapsed after leaders were arrested or exiled, or else succumbed to factional squabbling. A serious leadership problem existed, and the Russian model seemed to offer a solution for it.

In this general situation, Chen Duxiu, founder of *New Youth* magazine and possibly the leading intellectual of the New Culture movement, was approached by Russian agents searching for revolutionary allies. Chen previously had been a proponent of a long-term cultural approach to China's problems. But the events of May Fourth, and his own arrest and jail sentence for leafleting, convinced him that more immediate, political solutions were necessary. After three months in prison, he left Beijing for Shanghai to work with sympathetic young intellectuals in plotting a new strategy. It was in Shanghai that he met the Russians.

It was also in Shanghai that Mao Zedong, then working as a laundryman, sought Chen's support for the campaign against Zhang Jingyao. Although there are no accounts of these meetings, Mao did say later that Chen "had influenced me more than anyone else" at Beijing University. Now, again rather fortuitously, Mao found himself on the scene as plans were hatched for a Communist party. The first formal groups was organized in May 1920. Mao was probably a member (the history of this temporary grouping has been lost); certainly by the summer of 1920 he had become a Marxist. From that point on, his political convictions did not waver. And when he returned to Hunan, after the extirpation of Zhang Jingyao, its warlord, his Communist activities were based on firm conviction.

EARLY COMMUNIST ACTIVITY IN HUNAN

Chinese schoolmasters normally followed the relaxed lifestyle of scholars and gentlemen, drinking tea, composing verse, and occasionally tutoring a few students to get both disciples and extra funds. Schoolmaster Mao superficially fit this mold. He set up a "Self-Education College," opened the "Cultural Bookstore," and regularly devoted himself to intellectual discussions. But this veneer scarcely concealed the dynamo of political activity, who, along with the rest of his family, was busy organizing for the Communist cause.

As Mao wrote to his old friend, Cai Hesen, in Paris, "We must very carefully choose reliable people, sincere comrades." He already had a nucleus in his own family. His wife, Yang Kaihui, had been influenced by the new cultural currents in Beijing. His two brothers had been steeled by the fires of the May Fourth movement, as had an adopted cousin, now in Mao's charge after the death of his father. Around this radical core gathered the left wing of the New People's Study Society, about half of the original group of students from Hunan Normal School. The Self-Education College, whose advertisements appealed to penniless radicals who "wish to study but have no resources and are against the regulations in other schools," brought in more rebellious youth, while the Cultural Bookstore, stocked with revolutionary propaganda, helped them to locate many nonstudents who might have been overlooked.

By December 1920, Mao had built a firm-enough base to inaugurate formally a Hunan branch of the Socialist Youth Corps, the precursor to the Communist party. Promising members were sent off to the Soviet Union to work and study. Mao, however, remained in Hunan, where he continued to enlarge the youth corps, which reached a membership of 2,000 in 1922. From these were drawn the most reliable comrades to form the Communist party in July 1921. Mao and He Shuheng, both well known for their antiwarlord work as well as their Communist organizing, were natural choices as delegates.

When he returned from the Shanghai congress, Mao shifted the focus of his activities to labor organizing. During his spare time and on the relatively long school vacations, Mao the schoolmas-

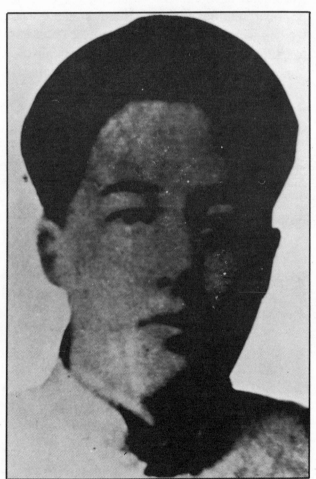

MAO ZEMIN (1896–1943), BROTHER.   MAO ZETAN (1905–1935), BROTHER.

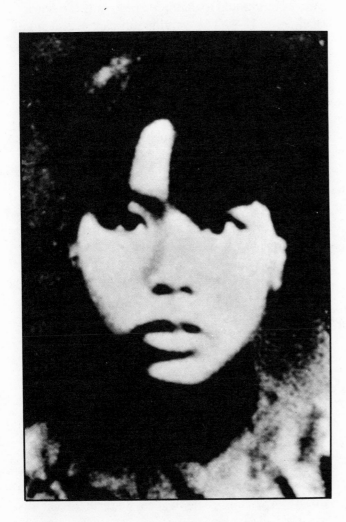

MAO ZEJIAN (1905–1929), ADOPTED SISTER.

"CHAIRMAN MAO GOES TO
ANYUAN"—A PAINTING.

ter, in his scholar's long gown and with a very proper paper umbrella, set off for Hunan's industrial areas to conduct the sort of social surveys that he had already carried out while at the normal school.

The conditions he found at the Anyuan coal mines, located to the southeast of Changsha along the main rail line, were appalling. The work day lasted fourteen or fifteen hours. Ventilation was so poor that the miners went naked underground. Wages amounted to pennies a day, only 26 "cash" or 8 cents U.S. The only health care was a small clinic for 6,000 workers. The workers had struck frequently against the German and Japanese capitalists who established the mines at the turn of the century, but they still had not formed a permanent organization.

On his first visit, Mao lodged with a family, from whom he learned many details of the miners' lives. When he returned that winter during semester break, he brought along his brother Zemin. Lodged in a small hostel, they helped the miners to organize a Communist cell. Mao then moved on to do similar work with railroaders and other workers. Zemin stayed on to develop cooperatives designed to break the grip of the company store and usurers on the miners. Mao returned in the spring to open a school for the miners' children and, eventually, the miners themselves. Books and papers from Changsha's Cultural Bookshop soon followed. When the workers organized a union and struck in September 1922, Mao and the Communist party were given credit for their success.

By late 1922 Mao chaired a federation of more than twenty unions and thousands of workers. They trusted him. Unlike most intellectuals, he happily sat and talked to them for hours. Even more surprisingly, he was not afraid to get his hands dirtied. He actually went down into the mines with the men, and inspected the hazardous conditions they showed him. Thus the workers felt they could rely on Mao when he represented them to the authorities.

All this was too much for the authorities. Zhao Hengti, the governor of Hunan, had formerly painted himself as a progressive. In the liberal climate after the expulsion of the former warlord, Zhao supported the right to organize, and even incorporated this right in a constitution which he personally drafted. Then his true colors began to show. When

AN ARTIST'S CONCEPTION OF MAO ADDRESSING THE ANYUAN MINERS.

AN OLD PHOTO OF THE 1922 ANYUAN MINERS' STRIKE. NOTE THE HALF–NAKED MINER ON THE RIGHT CARRYING HIS TOOLS.

workers at a state-owned textile mill struck, he recognized their demands, but, as a warning, executed the two strike leaders, members of the Socialist Youth Corps. Subsequently he refused to grant legal recognition to the miner's and railroaders' unions. Mao personally pleaded with him for this recognition and reminded him of the constitution. Mao's arguments failed to sway him, but did convince him that Mao was a dangerous subversive. He reportedly commented in December 1922, "This Mao is too clever. . . . There is not enough room in Hunan for both of us." In April 1923, after warlords elsewhere cracked down on the labor movement, Zhao ordered the arrest of Mao. Receiving warning in time, Mao escaped to Shanghai.

THE FIRST UNITED FRONT

When Mao arrived in Shanghai, the Communist party had just initiated a new strategy, a united front with the Nationalist party (also known as the Kuomintang or KMT) of Sun Yatsen.

The Nationalist party was less a political party than a clique of political personalities grouped around Sun Yatsen, who had been a major figure since the turn of the century. Sun had collaborated with foreign countries and conspired with secret societies in numerous fruitless efforts to establish a civilian government with himself at its head. Cooperation with Soviet Russia and the Chinese Communists was only a new chapter in a long book whose theme was Sun's personal leadership.

The Chinese Communists were familiar with the Nationalist party, and many, including Mao, opposed collaboration, since the older and larger party threatened to swallow them up and destroy whatever political identity they had formed in their first two years. But Comintern wishes for amalgamation prevailed as the labor movement around the country took a beating. The slaughter of fifty workers at a union meeting argued powerfully for the need to organize more broadly and develop self-defense. Cooperation with Sun meant a base in southern China and connection to a larger political network. Communists were convinced; they joined the Nationalist party as individuals, and few worked as enthusiastically as Mao to make the united front successful.

In January 1924, the Nationalist party was formally organized, with Communists holding many high positions. Mao held the post of alternate to the central executive committee. He returned from the congress in Guangzhou with the assignment to maintain liaison between the Communists and Nationalists of Shanghai.

For once, Mao had bit off more than he could chew. Politically sophisticated Shanghai did not respond to the calls for unity from above or from Mao. Right-wing Nationalists knew they had a stranglehold on the labor movement as long as Communist rank-and-file organizers could be kept out; they refused to cooperate with any threat to their power and privilege. Local Communists in turn would not abate their attack on corrupt union bosses and local politicians. Mao could not break this impasse. Exasperated and exhausted, he gave up after a year and quietly returned to his native village to recuperate.

MAO IN SHANGHAI, 1924.

THE RISE OF THE PEASANT MOVEMENT

Mao left Shanghai on the eve of momentous developments. Communist labor organizers had just established a base in the Japanese-owned textile industry. In the process of leafleting a factory, they clashed with Japanese guards, who shot and killed one of the organizers. Two weeks later, on May 30, a protest demonstration was fired upon by British police. The incident sparked a general strike which spread to all of China.

The May Thirtieth movement caught Mao unawares. Even more surprising was the militancy of the local peasants' response. But Mao, with several months' rest behind him, rapidly took command and organized a peasant branch of the Communist party in his own village in August. However, his activities brought him to the attention of Zhao Hengti, and once again he had to flee to avoid arrest.

Rather than return to Shanghai, Mao went to Guangzhou, the seat of Nationalist power in the south. As a Nationalist party leader, he was made editor of their *Political Weekly,* which he used as a forum to attack the Nationalist right wing. He held this position until the spring of 1926, when a major party shakeup purged the Communists from key leadership posts.

During this time, Mao also developed and consolidated his earlier efforts at peasant organizing by working at the Peasant Movement Training Institute founded by Peng Pai, the brilliant Cantonese organizer who first perceived the importance of the peasant movement to the Chinese revolution. Under Peng Pai's leadership, the institute graduated well-trained organizers, all Cantonese. Mao's crucial contribution was to broaden the institute's base by bringing in peasant leaders from all over China, especially Hunan, thereby laying the groundwork for a national movement.

The peasant movement played a major role in the summer of 1926, when the Nationalists attempted to reunify China militarily. Mao described the movement as "colossal," and expected that it would soon be "like a mighty storm, like a hurricane, a force so swift and violent that no power, however great, will be able to hold it back." Mao's expectations were premature; the mighty hurricane

MAO IN GUANGZHOU, 1925.

did not come for twenty more years. But the gale of 1926 gave a preview of what was to be.

In Hunan, newly formed peasant associations, some spawned by Mao's earlier organizational work, "settled accounts" with the landlords. Notorious villains who had brutally murdered peasants were now brought before tribunals to be tried and executed. Others "banished" themselves from the area rather than face peasant justice. Minor offenders were paraded around the village in tall paper hats with mottoes indicating their crimes. By shaming them, the peasants thought they would destroy the landlords' power.

Freed from outside control, the peasants also proceeded to reorganize village life. Consumer cooperatives and new distribution networks replaced the markets controlled by landlords and merchants. The problem of credit, which was often used to hold the peasants in bondage, was now resolved by cheap and easy loans from the cooperatives. Other problems, like gambling, opium

REVOLUTIONARY CARTOON. MODERN WOMAN CARRYING FLAG MARKED WOMEN'S LIBERATION CHASES AWAY IMPERIALISM, WARLORD, OLD LEARNING, AND BUREAUCRAT.

SHANGHAI'S ARMED WORKERS DURING THEIR BRIEF VICTORY.

smoking, and gluttony, became subject to community censure and disappeared—at least from public view.

Mao wrote up these events in his "Report on an Investigation of the Peasant Movement in Hunan," which contains one of his most famous remarks. Against those who claimed the revolution was going too far, he argued, first, that the landlords' crimes merited such punishment:

"Second, a revolution is not a dinner party, or writing an essay, or painting a picture, or doing embroidery; it cannot be so refined, so leisurely and gentle, so temperate, kind, courteous, restrained, and magnanimous [these last are the five Confucian virtues]. A revolution is an insurrection, an act of violence by which one class overthrows another. A rural revolution is a revolution by which the peasantry overthrows the power of the feudal landlord class....

"To put it bluntly, it is necessary to create terror for a while in every rural area, or else it would be impossible to suppress the activities of the counter-revolutionaries in the countryside or to overthrow the power of the gentry. Proper limits have to be exceeded in order to right a wrong, or else the wrong cannot be righted."

Among the wrongs that needed to be righted was the injustice to women. For Mao, the authority of the husband, and that of the state, the clan, and religion, formed four "thick ropes" binding the Chinese people. Those bindings were now being loosened. Momentary terror to accomplish these goals was acceptable to Mao. The landlords disagreed, as did many in the Nationalist party.

DIVISION AND BETRAYAL

Mao had predicted the revolutionary potential of the peasantry in 1925, when he also observed that the "intermediate classes are bound to disintegrate quickly, some sections turning left to join the revolution, others turning right to join the counter-revolution, with no room for them to remain 'independent.'" The development of the revolution dramatically bore out these predictions.

In the countryside, no landlord was safe, regardless of his revolutionary connections. Li Lisan, one of the early Hunanese Communists and the leader of the 1925 Shanghai general strike, had an old father, a landlord, who came to him for protection from the peasant association. Li dutifully wrote a letter assuring that his father would recognize and obey the peasant association. But the letter proved a poor talisman; after the old man left his son, he was never heard from again. Li remained a loyal Communist, but the general effect of this and similar events on the Nationalist officer corps, composed largely of landlords' sons, was unquestionably negative.

In the cities, Chinese capitalists came under attack. Strikes and demands raised against foreign companies for patriotic reasons soon spread to Chinese firms because of simple economics. The foreign companies, usually more financially secure than their hard-pressed Chinese competitors, could and often did pay their workers more. Strikes only exacerbated these differences, causing workers in Chinese firms to raise similar demands. Moreover, like the peasants, the workers used the new political climate to organize on a mass scale to right old wrongs, especially the workers of Shanghai, who were now at least partially armed after having seized power in the city from retreating warlord troops on March 21, 1927.

In these circumstances, the rich and powerful among the Chinese thought again about their support of the revolution. Yu Xiaqing, a powerful Shanghai banker and a prominent supporter of the Nationalist cause, approached Chiang Kaishek, the military leader of the Nationalist forces, in an attempt to get him to moderate revolutionary "excesses." Chiang, though regularly denounced in the foreign press as the "Red general" because of his Russian advisors and his public statements praising the Comintern, turned a sympathetic ear to the pleas of the propertied classes and their promises of financial support.

The revolution reached a crucial stage in Shanghai. The armed workers had welcomed the arrival of the Nationalist armies from the south, but refused to hand over their arms or disband their militia. They planned to follow the example of their comrades in Wuhan and seize the concessions, the areas of the city under foreign jurisdiction (almost three-quarters of Shanghai). One attempt had already been scheduled, but was foiled by the last-minute appearance of Chiang Kaishek, who urged the crowd to wait. It was only a matter of time before the workers consolidated their pow-

SOME OF THE ARMED WORKERS WHO SEIZED THE FOREIGN CONCESSIONS IN HANKOU IN 1927.

er and were able to act independently.

At this point, in a private meeting kept secret for twenty years, the French concession's chief of police brought together the American "mayor" of the large international concession and Shanghai's leading gangster, Du Yuesheng. They agreed that, with French arms and ammunition, Du's men would gather in the concession area, and from there launch a surprise attack on the workers' headquarters.

From their plot came the stunning *coup d'etat* of April 12, 1927 which catapulted Chiang Kaishek to political supremacy and turned the revolution in a rightward direction. The Communists were purged from the Nationalist party. The mass movement, when not directly suppressed, was relegated to almost an afterthought. The struggle against imperialism was channeled into the relatively innocuous course of treaty revision. This "moderation" came at an extremely high cost.

In Shanghai, 5,000 workers were left dead in the streets after the combined assaults of Du's gangsters and Chiang's troops. In Guangzhou, Soviet diplomats were slaughtered. In Beijing, Li Dazhao, the Communist party's intellectual mentor, was strangled to death. In Changsha, troops attacked protesting crowds in an unrestrained orgy of violence. But perhaps the most sadistic brutality happened in the countryside, where landlords who had been shamed with tall hats retaliated with murder and mutilation. A student activist in one village was covered with kerosene and burned alive. Peasants in another village suffered the "death of a thousand cuts," a prolonged agony of salt- and sand-infected wounds. Liberated women suffered most of all. A horrified witness observed as they "cut open the breasts of the women comrades, pierced their bodies perpendicularly with iron wires, and paraded them naked through the streets." All this was done in the name of curbing revolutionary "excesses."

Communist leaders in Wuhan, allied with anti-Chiang Nationalists, failed to lead an effective counterattack, hoping against hope that Chiang would be isolated and that "moderate forces would preserve the united front. Only when these Wuhan Nationalists conceded defeat and joined with Chiang, did the Communists go into opposition. As Mao had predicted, there was no room to be

SOME OF THE EXECUTED COMMUNISTS.

CHIANG KAISHEK, 1927.

LEADERS OF THE AUTUMN HARVEST UPRISING. MAO IS THIRD FROM THE LEFT.

independent of the peasant movement. The Communists had to leave the government and rejoin the popular movement.

THE AUTUMN HARVEST UPRISING

In a series of rapid moves, a new strategy was planned. The main Communist forces were to head downriver and south to establish a new revolutionary center in Nanchang. While they consolidated a military and political base there, Mao and other peasant leaders were to revive the movement in the countryside. With luck, they believed, the tide could be turned.

Accompanied by his brother Zetan, Mao set off for Hunan. First he contacted the Anyuan miners to form a politically reliable core. He then added elements of peasant self-defense militia and still revolutionary army troops. In all, he collected 8,000 troops into four regiments to form the First Division of the First Peasant and Workers Army. The task was not an easy one.

Early on, he had to travel on foot between the different units before they were pulled together into an effective force. This meant crossing hostile territory; so it was not long before landlord troops captured him. These particular troops decided against shooting him on the spot. Instead they took his shoes (to prevent his escape and to use themselves) and led him along with other captives back toward headquarters, no doubt hoping to get some reward. Mao took the troops' measure and concluded they were only interested in money. He borrowed as much as he could and tried to bribe his way free. He failed; the soldiers may have sensed there was a price on his head.

Mao's situation became desperate as they came within sight of the headquarters. He gambled on a sudden dash across a field. His years of physical hardening paid off: barefoot, he outraced the armed soldiers to some high grass near a pond, where he successfully eluded their search. When night fell, he set out over rocky terrain, stopping only when he found a friendly peasant who bound his blistered feet and bought him new shoes. Penniless but refreshed, he continued on to his original destination.

Mao's troubles did not end with his escape. Despite its grand name, the First Division of the First Peasant and Workers Army was very unlike a regular army. Uniforms (for those who had them) were mismatched, and shoes were often flimsy cotton. Mao wore no uniform and only plain straw sandals. Weapons were mostly pikes and spears; rifles were few and far between, and bullets were in short supply. Nevertheless, these troops valiantly began a series of uprisings in early September and scored some major victories.

AN ARTIST'S CONCEPTION OF THE FIRST PEASANT AND WORKERS ARMY.

1927-1935

THE RETREAT INTO THE MOUNTAINS WAS PROBABLY NOT AS RESOLUTE AS THIS MODERN PAINTER
ENVISIONED IT.

THE RED ARMY

"Do we dare to carry on the revolution?" Mao's words resounded in the village schoolyard. From a thousand throats came the reply: "We dare!" They were the remnants of the Autumn Harvest Uprising, and upon them depended the fate of the revolution. Mao was indomitable, but would they follow? He planned to lead them to the mountain fastness of Jinggangshan, a sparsely populated and easily defensible plateau more than 5,000 feet high on the border between Hunan and Jiangxi. They agreed; and so on September 20, 1927, the entire group set off for its new home.

On September 23, within sight of Jinggangshan, two hundred took measure of the task ahead and refused to go any farther. Mao knew his only power lay in persuasion. He let them go, and even offered travel money to anyone in need. The rest of the troops decided to stay, and continued the slow trek through the red-clay foothills. In the autumn rains, the soil turned into a sticky mud, and fires became impossible. At Liushi, a small market town, they just barely fought off an assault by Nationalist troops. Only when they reached the base of the mountain could they pause to rest and regroup.

Mao at this point looked very much like a bandit leader. Gaunt and ragged with shoulder-length hair, he must have terrified the local peasants as he came up to them. But when he asked them, "Cousin, what is your name?" their fears lessened, and they marveled at his talk of a people's army which came to serve them and not to loot. In this way he won their support, and gradually even the women and children in hiding came out to cook for and play with the soldiers.

Eventually even actual bandits joined up with Mao. Wang Zuo, a tailor, and Yuan Wencai, a former student, had followed checkered careers which had brought them into the Nationalist army during the peasant movement of 1926. When the landlords counterattacked, they fled to the hills and lived like bandits, preying on the people. When Mao arrived with his troops, they merged forces. This merger nearly doubled the Red Army, and brought a small supply of rifles, many badly in need of repair—but the bandits also brought their bandit ways.

The arrival of Wang and Yuan emphasized a problem already plaguing the Red Army. The soldiers of worker and peasant background were all simple folk whose hearts were in the right place, but whose culture poorly prepared them for the rigors of guerrilla war. Like other countries, China had its share of romantic brigands who laid waste the countryside in the name of higher principles: Robin Hoods who in theory robbed the rich to give to the poor, but in fact robbed the poor to give to themselves. Mao himself as a boy had greatly admired these heroes of China's past, but as a man and a revolutionary he recognized their failings.

From the very start, Mao remedied the bandit mentality with education. Many would have insisted on discipline alone, but Mao recognized that revolutionaries were motivated by ideals, and that the correct way to guide a revolutionary army was by means of ideological struggle which would criticize mistaken ideas. Moreover, if the troops were to survive, they had to "swim like fish through the sea of the people." They had to have the people's voluntary support, which would be offered because of a positive political rapport. Roving bandits may have been admired, but always at a distance. Revolutionaries had to work directly with the people.

The first months on Jinggangshan were very hard for the Red Army. Supplies were short. Discipline was poor. Despite Mao's directives, some troops did loot during the first attack on a town. This soon ended, as the soldiers absorbed the meaning of Mao' message. "Down with capitalism, eat squash" was the way they summarized the attack on the landlords; they refrained from seizing the peasants' rice, relying on the landlords' squash instead. In February, as soon as there was a bit of a thaw, Red Army men went out to help the peasants with the sowing and to reclaim land for their own needs. Self-sufficiency would remove the pressures that promoted banditry and would forge closer ties with the peasants.

During all these months, Mao was out of touch with the party. In the confusion after Chiang Kaishek's coup, he had gone off with his brothers and adopted sister to organize the Autumn Harvest Uprising. His wife and small sons had to be left in Changsha. On the run and in the mountains, he had to rely on the newspapers, which he read religious-

ZHU DE AND MAO ZEDONG.

ly, for information about the party's activities. Not until February or March, when a messenger reached his camp, did he learn that he was in disfavor with the party and had been dismissed from the political bureau. The insult of political isolation was now added to the injury of geographical separation.

Command was taken from Mao, and many of his troops were diverted south to fight warlord troops in a poorly planned insurrection. The attempt failed, and casualties were substantial. Meanwhile the Jinggangshan base was weakened and came under attack from local warlords.

At this critical juncture, Mao sent his brother Zetan to invite Zhu De to Jinggangshan. Zhu De, a short jovial Sichuanese in his early forties, led a desperate band of revolutionaries without a base who, in the spring of 1928, were facing imminent destruction. Zhu, with few options, decided to tie up with the beleaguered Mao. At the end of April, he and his troops reached the base of Jinggangshan. In a hard-fought battle, Mao's troops broke through the warlord encirclement of their base and cleared a path for Zhu De to advance up the mountain and join them. By a mountain stream the two men met and embraced, starting a lifelong collaboration.

Mao's alliance with Zhu De meant a significant political victory. Not only did Mao regain his base, but he also won an ally for struggles within the party. Zhu De had substantial revolutionary credentials, which included participation in the 1911 Revolution, membership in the Communist party since 1922, and a leading role in the Nanchang uprising of August 1927. Zhu was aware that Mao had been criticized. Nevertheless, he supported Mao and accepted partnership in control of a reorganized Red Army. Zhu De became military commander-in-chief and Zao served as political commissar of the renamed "Fourth Red Army," which was to form the core of Red power in China.

Mao convinced Zhu with arguments that have been preserved in the essay, "Why is it that Red political power can exist in China?" Mao's premise was that China's unique political situation, warlordism, which he described as "war within the White regime," created spaces where revolutionaries could survive. Moreover, these areas were not political vacuums, but places where the peasant movement had been very strong. The Red Army itself was an offshoot of the revolutionary forces of 1926–27. As long as revolutionary ferment continued, the Red areas would last, but they had to have a Red Army to cope with White forces, and a strong Communist party to give correct political leadership, especially in resolving economic problems.

Mao codified his ideas into simple slogans for the troops. The entire strategy of guerrilla war was reduced to four four-word phrases:

> "Enemy advances, we retreat.
> Enemy camps, we harass.
> Enemy tires, we attack.
> Enemy retreats, we pursue."

At the same time, new military standards were summarized into three rules of discipline and eight points for attention. In essence, these enjoined the Red soldiers not to loot, but to respect any villagers with whom they might be bivouacked. For example, if a soldier used a house door as his pallet, he personally was to rehang the door the next morning. By paying attention to these small details, the Red Army proved its claim of serving the people and won support for the revolutionary cause.

By their second winter on Jinggangshan, the Red Army had grown to number 4,000, twice the number of residents previously inhabiting the area. They strained the resources of the area. Mao conferred with Zhu De and they decided to head for the lowlands and a larger base. On January 14, 1929, soldiers were given a pound of rice each. With nothing other than the clothes on their backs and a few spare rounds of ammunition, the bulk of the army moved on to find a new base, while a smaller group remained behind to hold Jinggangshan.

For weeks the Red Army trudged through winter snows and rocky mountain passes. They kept away from towns and cities, but their presence became known. A far larger body of warlord troops got on their trail and were snapping at their heels. When they reached Dabodi, a small valley between Ruijin and Ningdu, Mao planned a counterattack. First he spread his troops through the surrounding hills; then he lured the warlord troops into the valley. Under the cover of afternoon fog and then all through the night, the fighting continued. By noon on February 11, the 7,000 enemy troops were defeated. Some 900 soldiers and 800 guns were captured. The victory laid the foundation for a new base area.

During the next few months Ningdu, then Ruijin, were captured. The Red areas developed beyond mere military garrisons, into genuine alternative governments. For example, when Ruijin was taken in May, Mao Zemin assumed control of the local bank to handle the more complex economic operations involved in running a city. By 1930, seventeen counties had Red governments. In November 1931, when a Soviet Republic was declared with its capital at Ruijin, Red rule extended over 19,000 square miles, encompassing a population of three million people.

MAO IN RUIJIN, 1931.

''Feeling expansive and the need for a few intimate companions, I one day inserted an advertisement in a Changsha paper, inviting young men interested in patriotic work to make contact with me. I specified youths who were hardened and determined, and ready to make sacrifices for their country. To this advertisement I received three and one-half replies.... The 'half' reply came from a noncommital youth named Li Lisan. Li listened to all I had to say, and then went away without making any definite proposals himself, and our friendship never developed.''

This was how Mao described the organization of the New People's Study Society and his first meeting with Li Lisan. A decade later, when Mao was consolidating his base in southeastern China, Li similarly was assuming control of the central party organs in Shanghai. The intervening years, however, did not bring about a meeting of the minds.

Li, a fiery orator with an exaggerated sense of self-worth, first made a name for himself during the May Thirtieth Movement, when he represented the Shanghai workers in strike negotiations. In 1928, at the Communist party's sixth national congress, held in Moscow, he was made director of propaganda, a task for which he was well suited. The Russians, who were directing the congress, intended him to be subordinate to Xiang Zhongfa, an ex-dockworker chosen to lead the party's new moderate strategy—a strategy which recognized the importance of Mao's efforts. But once back in China, Li asserted his authority and effectively displaced the docile Xiang. He pushed the party leftward and pressed for a general insurrection in the summer of 1930.

Mao became entangled in Li Lisan's schemes when he and Zhu De were ordered to take Changsha in August. Changsha, only a way station in Li's plan to capture Wuhan, had been seized earlier by Peng Dehuai, another Red Army commander, but then abandoned in the face of counterattacks by Chiang Kaishek's troops. The attack had gained three thousand recruits for the Red Army, but after their departure a White terror was unleashed. Any remaining leftists were arrested and killed. Mao's wife, Yang Kaihui, died during this onslaught, and his young son was arrested. The second attack

MAO ADDRESSING A PEASANT CONFERENCE, 1933.

SITE OF THE ZUNYI CONFERENCE.

came too late to save the victims of the White terror or to breach the walls of the city, heavily reinforced in the meanwhile. The city was besieged for nearly a month as Mao, Zhu, and Peng wrestled with the questions raised by Li Lisan's strategy. Then, in open disregard of his orders, they lifted the siege and returned south to Ruijin.

The Red Army commanders were not alone in their rebellion. The urban movement was decimated by futile insurrectionary attempts. By September their leaders were calling for Li's removal. The army's revolt only added fuel to these fires. By late September a full central committee meeting was called in Shanghai by Zhou Enlai, the highly respected mastermind of the 1927 Shanghai insurrections. Li Lisan was removed, but many of his policies were retained, causing the Russians to intervene directly in January and impose a new party leadership composed primarily of Russian-trained students.

While party squabbles continued in Shanghai, Mao faced a separate but similar problem in his Soviet base. The capture of the city of Jian brought to light an "anti-Bolshevik corps" created by the Nationalists to infiltrate and demoralize the Red areas. This group became associated with diehard followers of Li Lisan in the confused politics of the times. To sort matters out, Mao ordered the detention of 4,400 troops and the major party figures in Futian. In reprisal, other troops of the same army corps counterattacked to free their arrested comrades, thereby touching off several months of fighting. When it finished, hundreds were dead, and the Soviet regime was severely shaken.

All these struggles left Mao in an ambiguous position. Ignoring Li Lisan's orders and defeating the Futian rebels strengthened Mao's power in the Soviet area. When the formal Soviet government was inaugurated in November 1931 and elections were held, Mao received the most votes, thereby earning the title "chairman" (though it was his later election to the chair of the Chinese Communist party which made him best known as "Chairman Mao"). In this regard his actions seemed vindicated and his position secure. But in the eyes of the party's central committee, Mao remained an uncertain, rebellious figure. He had unilaterally gone against Li Lisan—Zhu De and Peng Dehuai were believed to have acted on his advice—and thereby broken party discipline. Moreover, although the central committee found Mao to have been correct about the Futian rebellion as an "antiparty, counterrevolutionary action," nonetheless they severely criticized his suppression of it, suggesting he had "arbitrarily" used it to incriminate his personal enemies. Thus from the very beginning, in 1931, Mao and the new party leadership, the "28 Bolsheviks," so-called because of their Russian training, were on a collision course. Having been independent, would he now submit to them? Would they use their party rank to seize control? Initially these questions went unanswered, overshadowed as they were by the looming threat of Chiang Kaishek.

THE ENCIRCLEMENT CAMPAIGNS

Developments in the Nationalist regime followed a complex route during these years. Chiang Kaishek, the apparent victor in July 1927, had to "retire" from office that August. He returned five months later, but for the following thirty months had to confront shifting coalitions whose only common enemy was he. Finally, in 1930, he emerged victorious from one last great confrontation. He then turned his attention to the Communists who, in part because of Li Lisan's insurrectionary attempts, once again posed a significant threat.

Chiang charted a series of "Anti-Bandit Annihilation and Encirclement Campaigns" in which the entire base area was surrounded and put under siege, like a head in a gradually tightening noose. The first, launched at the end of 1930, failed abysmally. The Communists used it to capture their first radio sets. The next spring, another failure for Chiang brought the Communists 20,000 prisoners and rifles. The third campaign, personally led by Chiang in command of an army ten times larger than the Red forces, was called off when popular pressure forced Chiang to respond to Japanese encroachments in Manchuria.

Then a totally unexpected development took place. Gu Shunzhang, the Communist head of security in the cities, was discovered while posing as a traveling magician. His arrest destroyed the entire urban underground. The central committee

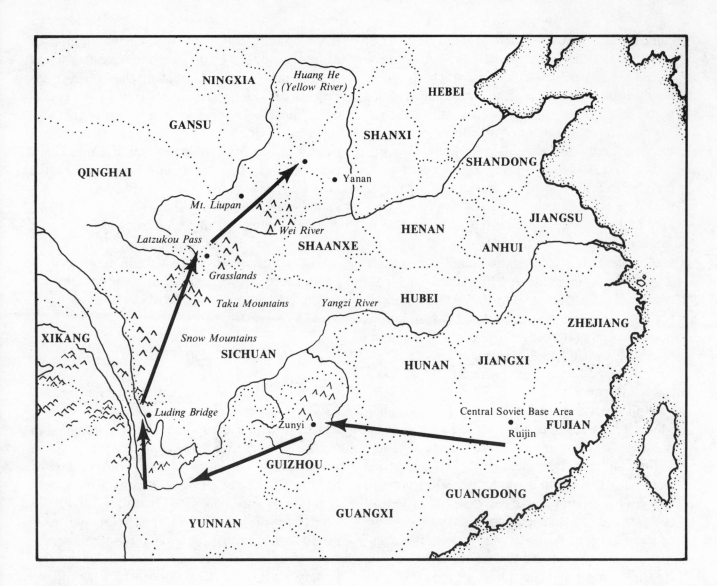

ROUTE OF THE LONG MARCH.

had to flee Shanghai. They headed for Ruijin, and once there confronted the obstreperous Mao Zedong directly. Immediately they moved to seize command. Zhou Enlai, the brilliant politician ultimately responsible for the party's military affairs, met Mao head on at a military conference in February 1932. Mao, for all his accomplishments, was no match for the suave and sophisticated Zhou. The power of the center was affirmed, and Mao's authority lessened.

Several month later, Mao's influence diminished further when he was bedridden with malaria. Hospitalized for four months, he watched helplessly as his brother Zetan was reprimanded for following traditional guerrilla tactics, and as other close allies like He Shuheng and Deng Xiaoping were criticized, all victims of a party shakeup designed to eliminate Mao's military strategy based on guerrilla war.

The new strategy of positional warfare, used by the party center to repulse the fourth encirclement campaign, brought no victories, only a tacit truce after eight months of fighting. Used again for the fifth campaign, it completely failed. Trying to hold ground against nearly a million troops, who had 400 airplanes and nearly unlimited munitions, proved to be an impossible task. After more than a year of last-ditch struggles, with conditions in the base areas barely tolerable, the Red Army was ordered to break out of the encirclement.

On October 18, 1934, Mao packed two blankets, an old overcoat and wool sweater, a battered umbrella, a bowl, and some books. He had just recovered from another bout with malaria during which his temperature had reached 105°. But this did not prevent him from setting out with his aide and his wife, a peasant Communist he married after Yang Kaihui's death. His brother Zetan was left behind, as were his children. The Long March had begun.

THE LONG MARCH

The Long March put a nation in motion. Men, women, and children, perhaps 100,000 in all, marched for a year, covering 6,000 miles over some of the most difficult terrain in China. Only 5,000 reached the final destination. But their survival ultimately guaranteed the success of the Communist movement in China.

The army-nation traveled on foot. When they set out, each soldier carried a five-pound ration of rice, a shoulder pole with ammunition or tools, and a pack with a blanket, warm uniform, and several pairs of cloth shoes with rope soles. Chopsticks were stuck into their leggings, and a needle with thread was carried in the visor of their caps. To guard against sun and rain, they had wide bamboo hats with a layer of oiled paper; many also had paper umbrellas. In addition, each carried a weapon, usually a rifle. Very little of this equipment survived the march intact.

The officers were supplied with the same equipment as the men. They were also assigned the few horses, but generally surrendered them to the sick and wound up walking most of the time. Mao, still weak from his bout with malaria, walked as soon as he regained his strength and covered the rest of the trip on foot except for a brief period when a relapse forced him into a stretcher.

Hiking the equivalent of the distance from New York to Los Angeles and back, by itself, was a major feat. But the more pressing concern on the Long March was not distance but attacks by Chiang Kaishek's troops, intent on wiping out the Communist "bandits" once and for all.

The first stage of the march proceeded rather simply. After careful secret planning, the Red Army suddenly struck out in a westerly direction, and after several bloody battles made it to Guizhou province, where some clever strategy and outright deceit—Red Army men dressed as Nationalists ran up to the city gate and demanded to be let in—put the town of Zunyi in their hands.

The capture of Zunyi allowed the Reds to stop and assess their situation. Almost half the troops had been lost in three months, and confidence in the "regular army" approach had waned. A party conference held in the town of Zunyi brought a major shakeup in the leadership, and Mao assumed command.

The Red Army, trimmed down to the bare essentials, began a series of distracting maneuvers intended to confuse Nationalist spotters flying overhead. As much as possible, they traveled at night to further prevent observation. The test of their strategy came in crossing the Yangzi.

The upper reaches of the Yangzi posed a formidable natural barrier to the Communist advance. Water pouring down for centuries from the Tibetan plateau toward the East China sea had carved out deep gorges amid great peaks rising up from impassable stone walls. In only a few places could the river be crossed at all. Knowing this, Chiang ordered troops on the north side to draw up and burn all the ferry boats, thereby guaranteeing the impossibility of any Communist escape. They were to be crushed between the river to their north and Chiang's troops advancing from the south. Chiang telegraphed his commanders: "The fate of the nation and the [Nationalist] party depends on bottling up the Reds south of the Yangzi."

The Communist counterstrategy depended on successful deception. First they made a feint to the

A SKETCH OF A GUIDE FROM THE YI NATIONAL MINORITY.

west, to make it appear that they would not try to cross the river. Then they turned back to the river, where they started work on a bamboo bridge. Chiang was pleased to get this news, for it meant they would be bogged down for several weeks, more than enough time for him to arrive with his troops. As Chiang organized the final attack, the real Communist plan was unveiled.

Some 85 miles downriver, at the only other ferry crossing in the area, the boats had been drawn to the other side but not burned. (Why waste good boats when the real battle was so distant?) By a forced march through the darkness of night and the hot, sticky day, a Communist battalion covered the distance to the ferry and surprised the local troops, capturing them without a fight. Through this small breach in the lines the Red Army poured for nine days and nights, escaping Chiang's clutches into the relative safety of the mountains of Xikang.

In the mountains they met tribesmen ordinarily hostile to the ethnic Chinese, but their organizing skills allowed them to win the tribesmen over easily and even gain recruits for the army. But this respite from Chiang's pursuit did not last long. They soon had to face the grave challenge of the Dadu river.

The Dadu had a long history of danger. Its icy rapids moved too fast to be navigated; even ferries at its slowest points faced great risks. The only safe crossings were over bridges made of iron chains or the very thickest of ropes. In the nineteenth century the fleeing Taiping rebels had delayed their crossing of the river and were massacred by Manchu troops as a result. Zhu De had heard stories in his childhood about the Taiping army and how they could be heard on moonless nights bewailing their fate. He, Mao, and the rest of the Red Army knew they had to beat Chiang to the river if they were not to meet the same fate as the Taipings.

Once again, by clever strategems, a small advance group made a surprise attack to seize a local ferry, but while troops lined up to cross, the river showed its strength. The rushing torrents slowed the small boats, until it was taking four hours to get even a few troops across. Meanwhile Chiang's planes arrived and added to the river's fury by bombing and strafing the troops.

Mao and the other leaders decided to gamble on the Luding bridge. A dozen miles upstream, thir-

THE BATTLE FOR THE LUDING BRIDGE, BY A MODERN PAINTER.

THE LUDING BRIDGE AS ONE OF THE LONG MARCHERS PERCEIVED IT.

teen iron chains installed in 1701 furnished the basic structure of a bridge. Ordinarily wood planks were laid over them, but Chiang's troops had removed these from the near side to the midway point. On the far side they set up a machine-gun nest as a further defense. The bridge appeared impassable and impregnable.

The Communists had little choice but to order a daring, desperate assault: 22 men, armed with rifles and hand grenades, after eating a nourishing meal to build up their strength, defied death by clinging to the chains, suspended between a rain of bullets and the raging river. Miraculouly they fought their way across, undeterred even by the final obstacle, a wall of flame ignited by the retreating Nationalist troops. The valor of these brave soldiers equaled that of the Spartans at Thermopylae, but was ultimately more important; for they, unlike the Spartans, accomplished their mission and saved the entire Red Army.

But even when the Red Army was saved from Chiang's pursuit, they next had to confront elements far more impersonal and implacable. To reach their goal of linking up with the Fourth Front Army under the command of Zhang Guotao, only

one hundred miles away, they still had the Great Snow Mountains to cross.

From 16,000 feet, the troops could see Tibet and feel the cold wind which cut through their ragged clothes. Hundreds died of exposure. Mao himself collapsed because of his malaria. The road trampled through the icy snow by the advancing army was marked by the bodies of the dead and dying, the warmth of their hearts snuffed out by the mountain's cold.

It was seven difficult weeks before the Red Army finally met up with Zhang Guotao's troops. The joy of the occasion diminished as the commanders began to feud over which way to head next. Mao wanted to continue on toward more populated areas, where the army could rely on peasant support. Zhang argued for falling back and seeking out Soviet Russia's aid. Compromise was reached, but the two armies pursued different paths.

Mao decided to head for Shaanxi province through a hole in the Nationalist lines, the Grasslands, an endless stretch of wild grass, soaked by rain in the summer and pelted with snow in the winter. Water and dead grass combined to form an evil-smelling swamp whose dank, foggy ecology

MARCHING THROUGH THE GRASSLANDS.

favored only the survival of giant mosquitoes.

The Red Army entered into this treacherous bog poorly equipped and short on supplies. Carefully holding on to ropes strung out by guides, they slowly advanced through the quicksandlike marsh. At night they slept standing up, back to back, to gain a little heat and to avoid slipping—and disappearing—in the mud. Many could not make it. One teeenage Red warrior announced, ''I am a piece of iron politically, but my legs fail me.'' He then collapsed and died the next day. Only after five or six hellish days did they finally emerge.

Back on more normal terrain, the Red Army still had a month to go before it reached its destination. For the exhausted soldiers, the threat of death was

ever present. Crossing Liupan mountain, Mao's orderly suddenly weakened and collapsed. When he came to, he found that Mao had covered him with his own overcoat and, standing exposed to the wind, stood watch while he recovered. He believed Mao saved his life. Mao may have, but certainly his own blood was warmed by the thrill of success. He wrote of that moment:

''On the high peak of Liupan mountain,
The Red flag ripples in the west wind.
Today the long rope is in our hands,
When shall we tie up the gray dragon?''

At last the Red Army reached Shaanxi. As it marched into the capital of the Northwest Soviet, crowds gathered with gongs and banners reading, "Welcome to Chairman Mao." Much like Henry M. Stanley, who fought his way through the jungle to find Dr. Livingston, Mao walked up to Xu Haidong, commander of the local Red forces, and asked, "Are you Comrade Haidong? Thank you for taking so much trouble to come here to meet us."

They had arrived.

HAPPILY DESCENDING THE MOUNTAINS.

1935-1949

MAO NOT LONG AFTER THE LONG MARCH.

"ROAR CHINA"—A CONTEMPORARY WOODCUT BY LI HUA FOR A PLAY PROMOTING THE UNITED FRONT.

THE SECOND UNITED FRONT

"Comrades! A great change has now taken place in the political situation. Our party has defined its tasks in light of this changed situation."

With the Long March over, the Communist party had to plan for the future. Its forces were reduced. A party that had ruled over millions now counted its supporters in the tens of thousands. The bases once spread throughout the country were reduced to one in China's barren northwest, where famine was almost as frequent as the dust storms that swept down from the Gobi desert.

Yet Mao refused to account this a failure. There were those in the party who argued that the Red Army had been defeated, but Mao compared them to the frog in the well who says, "The sky is not bigger than the mouth of the well." He went on to call the Long March "the first of its kind in the annals of history," and "a manifesto, a propaganda force, a seeding machine" showing that the Communists feared no difficulties or hardships.

Revolutionary victory, however, was not imminent. The Japanese threat to China's continued existence overrode other domestic political problems. China had to prepare for a protracted war against the mighty military machine of Japan, and required a united front of all patriotic forces. Revolutionaries had to open their doors to cooperation with their former opponents, and settle for the lesser goal of a "democratic revolution" directed against Japanese imperialism and its feudal collaborators in China.

Those were the tasks of the Communist party as

YANAN THEN.

YANAN TODAY.

CHINESE COMMUNISM'S TOP THREE: ZHOU ENLAI, ZHU DE AND MAO.

defined by Mao in December 1935, after two weeks of intense discussion by the political bureau of the central committee. Mao was now the titular head of the party, and his remarks were addressed to a conference of party activists in the tiny town of Wayaobao in northern Shaanxi province.

Mao was just 43 years old at the time. Sickness and struggle during the previous year had left him emaciated and gaunt. An American journalist who met him soon afterward thought he looked "Lincolnesque" because of his thinness, height, and mane of black hair. He also had trouble adjusting to the harsh climate and ways of the northwest. The local people used a heated bed, called a *kang,* which diverted cooking exhaust from the kitchen into the main room where it warmed a platform used for sleeping and even many daytime activities. Mao, however, continued to use a bed in the style of his native, semitropical Hunan—complete with mosquito net!

With the passing of time, Mao adjusted to his surroundings. A chain smoker, he tested many tobacco substitutes before he was able to grow his own. A lover of pepper like all Hunanese, he agreed to eat the local bread and millet, but only after arrangements were made to have red peppers baked in the loaves and cakes. Beyond these two concerns, Mao was little troubled, since much of his boyhood had been given over to toughening himself, and the Long March experience made even the barest quarters luxurious.

Mao's life-style at this time was extremely simple. In sparsely furnished rooms, decorated only by maps hung on the wall, he worked twelve to fourteen hours a day, writing articles and pamphlets outlining the political conjuncture and the party's response to it. Often he would work right through meals and into the night, surviving on a diet of cigarettes and tea. Between writing bouts, he wandered about the small community, mixing freely with the local peasants and on occasion being asked to sing at informal social gatherings.

He cared little about social propriety. He wore his hair long and shaggy, and his uniforms always looked unkempt. Edgar Snow, the American journalist who traveled to the Communist capital in 1936 and met with Mao, described him as having the manners of a Chinese peasant, which many would consider coarse and vulgar. He picked lice from his crotch in public, and once, while Snow was conducting an interview with the President of the Red Academy, stripped off his pants and lay on a bed to cool himself.

Mao paid far more attention to detail in political matters. His interviews with Snow document this abundantly. Mao went on at great length about political policies, but only answered questions about himself after some prodding. Snow remarked that Mao shared this trait with other Communists. In giving his autobiography, he "would be able to tell everything that had happened in his early youth, but once he had become identified with the Red Army, he lost himself somewhere, and without repeated questioning you could hear nothing more about *him,* but only stories of the Army, or the Soviets, or the Party—capitalized."

Snow's observation here must be tempered a bit by retrospective judgment. Mao and the other Communists had forged their views during fifteen years of difficult struggle. The resultant "party line" transcended particular individuals, yet inevitably became associated with single names. The policy of urban insurrection in 1930 was later known as the Li Lisan line," after the party official most associated with it. When Mao talked to Snow in very abstract terms about "the correct leadership of the Communist Party" and various "erroneous" policies in 1933 and 1934, he in fact was talking about himself and his struggles with opponents in those years.

Snow was no political innocent either. *Red Star Over China,* his account of his trip to the Communist base area and his interviews with its leaders, exceeded the demands of simple investigative journalism. Snow plainly supported the united front, calling for resistance to Japan. His glowing descriptions of life in the Communist areas were clearly intended to break down the Nationalist news blackout and to counter Nationalist propaganda, which was designed to picture the Communists as ogres and thereby frustrate potential unity.

In 1936 this blockade was the major fact of the Communists' existence. Mao, writing a textbook on military strategy, focused all his attention on Chiang Kaishek's encirclement campaigns. Chiang,

TEACHER AND STUDENT: MAO AND XU TELI, THEN 60, WHO HAD BEEN MAO'S HIGH-SCHOOL TEACHER TWENTY YEARS EARLIER AND LATER PARTICIPATED IN THE LONG MARCH.

MASTER AND PROTEGE: LIN BIAO, HERE ON MAO'S RIGHT, AS EARLY AS 1938 PRAISED "THE GENIUS OF COMRADE MAO'S LEADERSHIP."

confiding his thoughts to his diary, concentrated on the same campaign and expected to wipe out the Communists "in a couple of weeks or at most a month." The only glimmer of hope was the local Nationalist commander, a Manchurian simmering with patriotic anger after the loss of his father and his homeland to the Japanese. Known as the "Young Marshal," Zhang Xueliang had early on agreed to a truce with the Communists. (This truce, in fact, was the reason that Snow made it through the previously impenetrable blockade.) But in December 1936, Chiang came to the northwest to assume personal command of the final drive.

To the surprise of everyone, the previously docile Zhang Xueliang mutinied, and arrested Chiang Kaishek just as military operations were to start. This "Xian incident," named after the site of the mutiny, put the Communists in a delicate position. Chiang was and remained their mortal enemy; yet they mediated his release in the belief that only he could end the anti-Communist offensive and lead the resistance to Japan. Figures on the right were willing to risk his death; indeed, it was rumored that General He Yingqin wanted to remove Chiang as an obstacle to his own advance. Many on the left wanted to take revenge for Chiang's crimes in the

past, regardless of the consequences. The crisis simmered until finally the mutineers made a tacit agreement with Chiang and released him. Days later Mao issued a statement warning Chiang to respect the terms of the united-front agreement, but once Chiang was released there was little more that could be done.

For the next six months, united-front politics walked a tightrope between capitulation to Chiang Kaishek and a return to the former hostilities. Many thought the choices were exclusive: either a united front which accepted Chiang's dictatorship; or democracy, which made cooperation with Chiang impossible. Mao counseled that both were necessary.

Then Japan invaded. Initiated by the hawkish General Tojo, out of the Tokyo government's control, hostilities erupted late on the night of July 7, 1937. Chiang Kaishek tried to negotiate a settlement, but the Japanese countered with the invasion of Shanghai in August. While diplomats talked peace, the military juggernaut rolled on. Nanjing, the Nationalist capital, fell in December. Japanese troops raped, pillaged, and massacred a hundred thousand civilians. After this, anything less than resistance was unthinkable.

WRITER AND SUBJECT: EDGAR SNOW AND MAO.

THE NEW STAGE

After a year of fighting, the war settled into a stalemate. Japanese troops occupied ports and rail lines, and succeeded in forcing the Nationalists to retreat up the Yangzi valley to the mountain-ringed province of Sichuan. The countryside eluded their control. Guerrilla forces roamed freely, and organized their own ruling bodies to compete with the puppet government under the thumb of Japan.

Loss of the cities was nonetheless a major blow. Intellectuals and students who had been the core of the patriotic movement had to flee. Many went to Chongqing, the Nationalist wartime captial in Sichuan. The more leftist among them headed for Yanan, the Communist capital in Shaanxi.

This flood of refugees brought a major change to Mao's personal life. He had been married to a peasant Communist since 1930, when his previous wife was captured and beheaded by the Nationalists. This wife, He Zizhen (his third if the marriage arranged by his father is counted), bore him several children and accompanied him on the Long March, during which she was wounded by bomb shrapnel. In the fall of 1937, she became sick and had to be hospitalized in Moscow. Mao, suddenly independent and highly desirable, became the target of amorous intrigues among the newly arrived refugees.

Lan Ping, a Shanghai movie actress active in the patriotic movement, was one of the eligible and attractive young women participating in the agit-prop theatrical dramas put on in Yanan. How her relationship with Mao began and developed has been obscured by subsequent scandal. But their liaison grew serious enough for Mao to demand a divorce. This caused dismay over Mao's cavalier treatment of He Zizhen, and raised doubts about Lan Ping's motives (since the top leaders' wives usually also had prominent positions). Against strong objections, Mao was divorced in 1938 and after several months delay he married Lan Ping, who (possibly on Mao's advice) adopted a new name, Jiang Qing, to replace her stage name. (Her original family name was Li). The marriage was frowned on by the other Communist leaders; and to gain their approval, Mao had to agree that his new wife would have no public role, a promise kept until the onset of the Cultural Revolution. (He

A SOLITARY MAO IN YENAN.

HE ZIZHEN, MAO'S THIRD WIFE, SEEN TODAY WITH HER GRANDDAUGHTER.

OPPOSITE: MAO AND JIANG QING.

Zizhen meanwhile recovered and returned to China, where she is still living quietly today.)

Apart from these personal changes, the new stage brought a restructuring of the political situation which Mao had to analyze. Once again, as during the warlord period of the 1920s, China was divided between competing governments and armies. The Japanese army and puppet governments occupied the heartland, but the Nationalists, restricted largely to Sichuan, were recognized by the Allies and received aid from the Soviet Union and the United States. The Communists, because of the united front, were formally part of the Nationalist structure. The Red Army was reorganized into the Eighth Route and New Fourth Armies to fit into the Nationalist military structure. But formal incorporation still left the question of substantial control. Who was to control the Communist armies, and what was to be their political line?

Wang Ming, a Russian-trained theoretician who returned from Moscow in late 1937, promoted the policy of "everything through the united front" which carried the day during 1938, while Japanese troops pounded at the Chinese defenses. The severity of Nationalist and Communist military defeats, however, made many party leaders pause and give consideration to Mao, who argued for "unity and independence," or the preservation of Communist initiative within the united front, so that guerrilla warfare would be free to develop. By the end of 1938, mobile warfare successes and rumors of vacillation by Chiang combined to win a majority of party leaders to Mao's views.

It was during these years that the unique body of concepts known as "Mao Zedong thought" began to take shape. The guerrilla leader of earlier years had little chance to articulate theories, and his position in the party prior to 1935 forced him to follow orders as often as to give them. The Long March made him the first among equals, and peaceful conditions in Yanan gave him the opportunity to write, which he began to do in abundance.

His theme was people's war, or revolution as a "mass undertaking," in which "it is often not a matter of first learning and then doing, but of doing and then learning, for doing is itself learning." To prove his points, he would often cite old adages, such as "Nothing in the world is difficult for one who sets his mind to it" and "How can you catch tiger cubs without entering the tiger's lair?" This emphasis on practice was buttressed by deeper, detailed studies of Marxist epistemology and ontology. Always he returned to the importance of the masses. In November 1937 he wrote, "A war of partial resistance by the government alone without the mass participation of the people will certainly fail, . . . for it is not a national revolutionary war in the full sense, not a people's war."

These large and very complex concepts were not easily understood or accepted outside or within the Communist party. The Nationalist party was based on the idea of the "tutelary dictatorship" which would educate the people. Mao's concept reversed this priority; the government should follow the people instead of the people following the government. The Communist party more readily accepted guerrilla warfare based on popular mobilization, especially after 1938, but a massive educational movement was required before all the implications were mastered.

MAO CONVERSING WITH DR. ATAL, AN INDIAN DOCTOR SERVING THE REVOLUTIONARY CAUSE.

MAO, ZHU DE, AND AGNES SMEDLEY, THE AMERICAN REVOLUTIONARY.

MAO WRITING "ON PROTRACTED WAR" IN 1938.

MAO CHATTING WITH THE PEASANTS OF YANGJIALING.

"LITTLE RED DEVILS" FROM THE EIGHTH ROUTE
ARMY RECEIVE A LESSON FROM THEIR
COMMANDER.

THE RECTIFICATION MOVEMENT

By 1941 the Communist party faced several problems. A twentyfold growth in membership produced a party unwieldy in structure and uncertain in theory. Expansion of guerrilla forces led to open fighting with Nationalist troops. On January 4, 1941, the New Fourth Army headquarters were attacked, and of a group of 9,000, largely noncombatants, only 1,000 survived. Thus, to integrate the party and to prepare against any new offensive, the rectification movement was launched.

Yanan became one big school, studying works by Mao and other leading Chinese Communists, along with the recently published history of the Soviet Communist party written by Stalin. Soldiers and intellectuals discussed daily the evils of sectarianism, subjectivism, formalism, empiricism, dogmatism, doctrinairism, authoritarianism, bureaucratism, despotism, liberalism, semi-

anarchism, and other isms too numerous to mention. By the time they had finished, they had learned a new language and method which allowed them to focus precisely on any political problem.

The Yanan Forum on Art and Literature, held in May 1942, stands out as one of the more important moments in the entire rectification process. Literature and art had all along been closely tied to the patriotic struggle but still followed their own paths, as writers and artists sought out new forms to express their ideas. Naturally, great divergences and heated disputes arose among the artists, all ostensibly sharing the same political goals. Mao tried to resolve the arguments by posing a simple test: "For whom?" Lu Xun, China's greatest twentieth-century writer, had already answered this six years earlier, just before his death:

"A common aim is the prerequisite for a united front. . . . The fact that our front is not united shows that we have not been able to unify our aims, and

A CLASS BEING TAUGHT BY MAO.

OPPOSITE: MAO ADDRESSES THE ANTI–JAPANESE MILITARY AND POLITICAL COLLEGE ON THE OCCASION OF ITS THIRD ANNIVERSARY.

THE YANAN FORUM ON ART AND LITERATURE. MAO IS SEATED IN THE CENTER OF THE FRONT ROW.

OPPOSITE: MAO AT THE YANAN FORUM ON ART AND LITERATURE.

A YANAN CLASSROOM. THE BLACKBOARD HAS WRITTEN ON IT IN TRANSCRIPTION AND CHARACTERS "DOWN WITH JAPANESE IMPERIALISM!"

LU XUN AND G.B. SHAW, CIRCA 1920.

that some people are working only for small groups or indeed only for themselves. If we all aim at serving the masses of workers and peasants, our front will of course be united."

The Yanan Forum under Mao's aegis established the ''mass line'' in literature and art, by following Lu Xun's injunction to serve the masses of workers and peasants. The following year Mao laid down the principle: "In all the practical work of our party, all correct leadership is necessarily 'from the masses, to the masses.' " These ideas had a shattering effect on elitist and careerist party members, and tens of thousands resigned. However, many peasants and workers were now encouraged to join. By 1944 membership exceeded that in 1941 and continued to increase; it reached well over a million by April 1945, the end of the campaign.

Perhaps the most enduring consequence of the rectification campaign came at its peak in 1943, when Liu Shaoqi, Zhou Enlai, and other party leaders began to praise ''Mao Zedong thought.'' In July Liu, chief of the underground in the Japanese-controlled areas, advised all party members to ''arm themselves with Comrade Mao Zedong's thought.'' In August Zhou Enlai, the party's main representa-tive in Chongqing, returned to Yanan and an-nounced, ''Comrade Mao Zedong's ideas, through-out the entire history of the party, have developed into a Sinified Marxism-Leninism and are thus the line of Chinese Communism.''

Mao Zedong thought laid the basis for the per-sonality cult which soon had Mao being described by peasants as the ''savior of the people.'' Behind these extravagant claims lay a more comprehen-sive political move intended both to combat Chiang Kaishek's claims as the sole figure of national unity and to compensate for Stalin's dissolution of the Comintern. The 1936 Xian incident had re-vealed Communists' dependence on even a reluc-tant Chiang Kaishek for the national united front, and in a 1939 testimonial Mao had rhetorically asked, ''If we did not have Stalin, who would give the orders?'' So in the summer of 1943, when Stalin dissolved the Comintern to placate Churchill and Roosevelt, the Communist party seized the opportunity to elevate Mao as a national leader and to promote Mao Zedong thought as an indigenous theory appropriate to Chinese developments. Of course, once this course was set upon it led to consequences unsuspected at the start.

MAO MAKING A POINT TO CADRES DURING THE RECTIFICATION MOVEMENT.

SELF-RELIANCE: TROOPS THRESHING WHEAT.

LOST CHANCE IN CHINA

A major Japanese offensive in 1944 renewed pressure for the united front. The Americans, in the war since Pearl Harbor and by 1944 the major source of supplies for the Chongqing government, now attempted the previously impossible task of unifying all of China's armies—only this time it would be under American command. Preliminary to the final reorganization, an American military-observer group was assigned to Yanan. The Dixie Mission, called such because it was going into "rebel" territory, left Chongqing in July 1944.

Attached to the group was a young Foriegn Service officer born in China and fluent in Chinese, John Service. He was well acquainted with the Chinese scene, but had had no real dealings with the Communists. He had heard good stories about Yanan, but felt there had to be a "catch" somewhere. His doubts dissolved in the first favorable impressions of Yanan, which he wrote up in a report:

"Relations of the officials and people toward us, and of the Chinese among themselves, are open, direct, and friendly. Mao Zedong and other leaders are universally spoken of with respect (amounting in the case of Mao to a sort of veneration), but these men are approachable, and subservience toward them is completely lacking. They mingle freely in groups....

"There are also no beggars, nor signs of desperate poverty....

"Women not only wear the same clothes (trousers, sandals or cloth shoes, and often a Russian-type smock), they act and are treated as friendly equals....

"There is everywhere an emphasis on democracy and intimate relations with the common people of this area....

"But recreation is encouraged....At the dinner

SELF–RELIANCE: SPINNING COTTON IN YANAN.

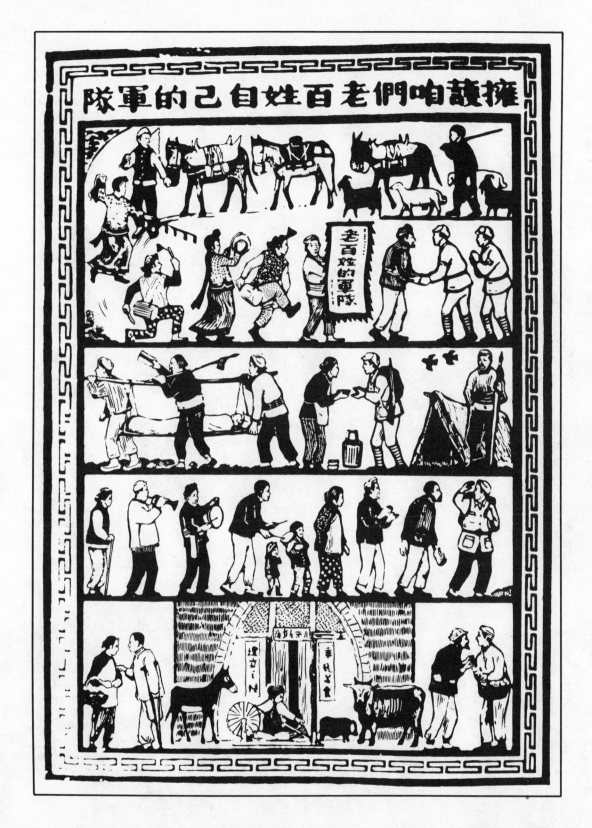

ABOVE: SEEKING POPULAR SUPPORT: THIS WOODCUT URGES "SUPPORT OUR COMMON PEOPLE'S OWN ARMY."

OPPOSITE, TOP: SELF-RELIANCE: BACKYARD FURNACE IN YANAN.

OPPOSITE, BOTTOM: BY THE END OF THE WAR, THE MANY COMMUNIST AREAS WERE PRINTING THEIR OWN BANKNOTES. MAO'S PICTURE WAS USED ON THE 500-YUAN NOTE.

GUERRILLA WAR COULD BE FOUGHT BY SOLDIERS ON HORSES DURING THE DAY.

GUERRILLA WAR WAS ALSO FOUGHT BY PEASANTS TEARING UP RAILROAD TRACKS AT NIGHT.

MAO'S OFFICIAL PHOTO AT THE END OF THE WAR.

WHEN LORD MOUNTBATTEN (IN NAVAL UNIFORM) VISITED CHINA IN 1943, CHIANG KAISHEK AND HIS
WIFE WERE VERY PLEASED TO RECEIVE ENGLAND'S SUPPORT. GENERAL STILWELL (ON THE RIGHT) MAY
HAVE BEEN LESS OPTIMISTIC.

THE AMERICAN AMBASSADOR TO CHINA, PATRICK HURLEY, VISITED YANAN. HERE HE IS GIVEN A
GUIDED TOUR BY MAO.

given for us just after our arrival, all the most important leaders joined in the dancing in the most natural and democratic manner.''

Dancing, however, was not the purpose of Service's presence. He was to sound out the Communists' political views, and to do so he interviewed Mao. Mao, surprisingly, praised American democracy and promised to cooperate with the United States, even better than the Nationalists did. He explained that civil war was "inevitable but not quite certain," and implied that the decision whether there would be a civil war lay in American hands. The Soviet Union had taken too much of a beating in the war to exert much influence. Only the United States had the resources to help China. Those resources could be used to promote economic reconstruction or military destruction. Mao closed the interview with almost a plea:

"America does not need to fear that we will not be cooperative. We must cooperate, and we must have American help. This is why it is so important to us Communists to know what you Americans are thinking and planning. We cannot risk crossing you—cannot risk any conflict with you.''

Service considered Mao sincere. From his own experience he could see the logic in Mao's argument, and knew that in any case the Communists would remain a major political force in China. He recommended that the United States actively support reform. But this was not to be.

Military reorganization was skillfully sabotaged by Chiang, who maneuvered Patrick Hurley, a wealthy Oklahoma lawyer acting as President Roosevelt's personal representative, into supporting Chiang against General Stilwell, the proposed American commander. Hurley then convinced

AT THE SEVENTH PARTY CONGRESS IN APRIL 1945, MAO ANNOUNCED THE COMMUNISTS' SUPPORT FOR A DEMOCRATIC COALITION GOVERNMENT AFTER THE WAR.

Roosevelt to remove Stilwell. When Stilwell departed, so did the idea of an overall American command.

Hurley followed up with personal mediation efforts. He flew to Yanan and met with Mao, who agreed to a five-point plan for a coalition government. Mao appreciated this effort, and wrote to President Roosevelt praising Hurley. Chiang Kaishek, however, rejected the five-point plan, and countered with his own three points. Mao ridiculed this new proposal that the Communists give up their armies without prior guarantees: "These people say to the Communists, 'If you give up your army, we shall give you freedom.' If these words were sincere, then the parties which had no army should have enjoyed freedom long ago."

The survivor of Chiang's 1927 coup and the 1935 Long March could not so easily forget. Yet Hurley failed to understand this long history of bitter struggle. To him the Communists were merely "outs who wanted to be in, and . . . the only difference between Oklahoma Republicans and Chinese Communists was that the Oklahoma Republicans were not armed." Consequently, Hurley backed off from the agreement which he had signed and resumed his unconditional support of Chiang. Once again the United States lost a chance to unify the Chinese forces and prevent a civil war.

CIVIL WAR

The atomic implosion at Hiroshima on August 6, 1945, announced a new age and propelled Chinese domestic affairs into a new stage. The Communists, who began the war with no more than 60,000 soldiers and limited territorial control, now could boast one million regular army troops, twice as many in the militia, and a dependent population of 100 million spread through the Chinese countryside. In Japanese-occupied cities, a Communist underground flourished in the factories. Chiang Kaishek, on the other hand, emerged from the war with at least five million men in his own army and received support from 50,000 American Marines and the entire Japanese occupation army. Both sides' forces were immense. A civil war would be devastating and politically unacceptable to war-weary China.

MAO TOASTS CHIANG KAISHEK IN THE HOPE OF WINNING A POLITICAL AGREEMENT.

Mao ventured into the tiger's lair to negotiate a postwar settlement. Two weeks after the Japanese surrender, Mao, accompanied by Hurley to guarantee his safety, flew to Chongqing for six weeks of negotiations peppered with parties and nights at the opera. Superficially, the mood was promising. Mao even toasted Chiang Kaishek and wished him a long life. In the formal talks he conceded control of territory in the south, and agreed to reductions in Communist armed forces which would have given the Nationalists a 7:1 superiority. But underneath Mao remained firm and defended essential Communist gains. Chiang, too, had not forsaken his principles, and remained intent on final victory. The final communiqué stressed peaceful postwar reconstruction, but offered little in the way of concrete proposals.

The Communists at this point did not want civil war. Quite simply, as one put it, they were quite sure they would not lose, but they were not so certain that they could win. Conversely, Chiang wanted to strike before any compromises weakened his hand. Using American troops and planes, he shuttled half a million of his best-equipped soldiers into Manchuria. Meanwhile, other divisions forced their way into Communist areas further south. Chiang's American chief of staff advised against these moves because he expected resistance. He was right. Fighting broke out at the end of 1945.

Washington at this time weakened its support for Chiang. It too opposed the civil war. President

OCTOBER 1945, MAO RETURNED TO YANAN AND A TUMULTUOUS WELCOME.

WITH THE WARTIME BLOCKADE LIFTED, CONDITIONS IN YANAN IMPROVED. HERE MAO STANDS BEFORE HIS "STAFF CAR" INSCRIBED IN ENGLISH AND CHINESE: "TO THE HEROIC DEFENDERS OF CHINA FROM THE CHINESE HAND LAUNDRY ALLIANCE, NEW YORK CITY."

ABOVE: PEACE DID NOT COME TO POSTWAR
CHINA. WHEN AMERICAN PLANES WERE USED TO
TRANSPORT CHIANG'S TROOPS, CHINESE
STUDENTS IN SHANGHAI DEMONSTRATED
AGAINST THE AMERICAN MILITARY PRESENCE.

RIGHT: THE FLIGHT FROM YANAN: ON FOOT.

THE FLIGHT FROM YANAN: ON HORSEBACK.

OPPOSITE: CIVIL WAR BROUGHT RENEWED DEVASTATION. HERE CHILDREN LINE UP FOR FOOD.

FOLLOWING PAGES: AS CHIANG'S GOVERNMENT COLLAPSED, A PANIC HIT THE CITIES. HERE SHANGHAI RESIDENTS PRESS IN LINE TO BUY GOLD.

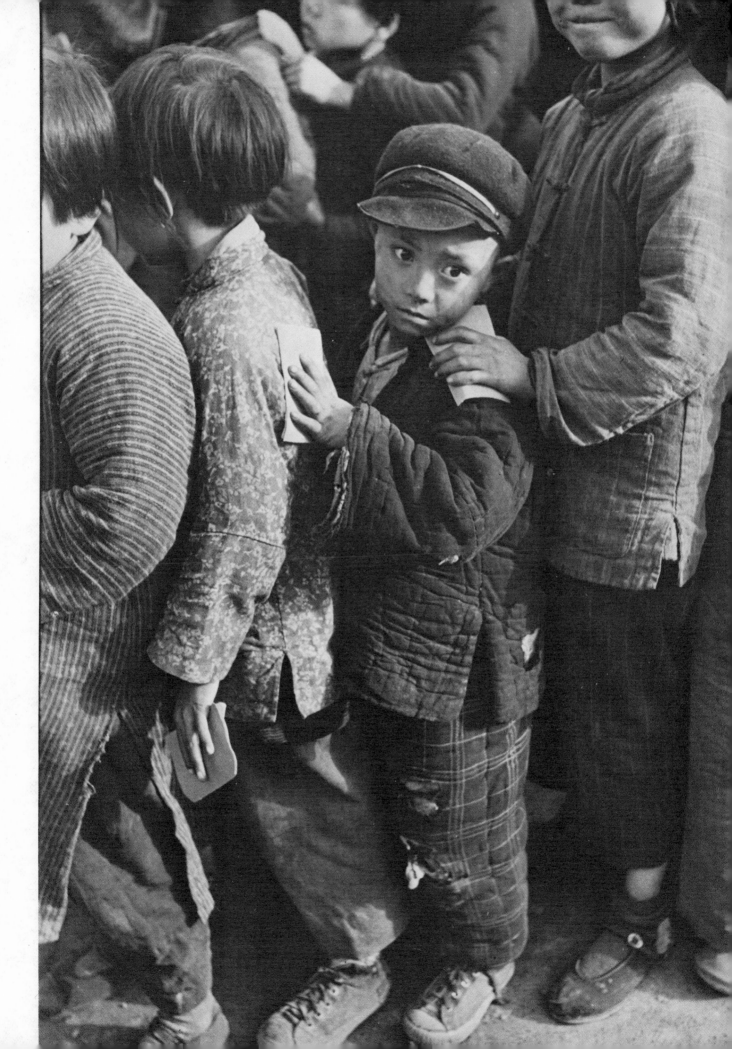

SPRING 1949: COMMUNIST TROOPS CROSS THE YANGZI INTO SOUTHERN CHINA.

THE VICTORIOUS TROOPS POSE ON THE ROOF OF CHIANG KAISHEK'S FORMER PRESIDENTIAL PALACE IN NANJING.

Truman sent General George Marshall, the architect of European reconstruction, to China to mediate. Chiang, still dependent on American aid, consented to a ceasefire. When Marshall left China temporarily in the spring of 1946, Chiang resumed his offensive. He explained to Marshall on his return, ''It was first necessary to deal harshly with the Communists, and later, after two or three months, to adopt a generous attitude.'' Marshall forced a new truce in July, but cold-war sentiment in the United States did not allow the even-handed approach necessary to avert civil war. Marshall's credibility soon declined, and he left China in January 1947, blaming ''irreconcilable groups'' in the Nationalist party for their ''feudal control of China'' and, to be even-handed, the Communists for their ''unwillingness to make a fair compromise.'' But could the Communists have accepted their own destruction?

From mid-1946 to mid-1947, the Communists were pushed back. Yanan had to be evacuated in March 1947. Mao set out on a new ''Long March'' across northern Shaanxi to set up a temporary base. but his long march brought more than survival. In less than a year, victory in the whole of China was in sight.

Military figures tell the story. When the war began, in 1946, the Communists were outnumbered five to one. By mid-1947 Communist forces had doubled, those of the Nationalists had shrunk. Still, it was about two to one. Further Communist growth and Nationalist losses evened the armies by late 1948. By this time Chiang's control was shattering. Troops deserted. Whole divisions joined the Communist ranks. In January 1949 Chiang himself resigned and fled the country. By April 1949, when the Nationalist capital of Nanjing was taken, a massive People's Liberation Army of four million troops confronted far smaller forces, staggering and in retreat.

On October 1, 1949, with fighting still going on in the south and areas like Taiwan completely out of control, Mao announced the establishment of the People's Republic of China. Economic reconstruction could not await the final resolution of the fighting. The Chinese people, Mao said, had ''stood up,'' and now they had to move on.

SUMMER 1949: MAO AND ZHU DE (TO MAO'S LEFT) IN BEIJING.

FOLLOWING PAGES: THE LIBERATION OF SHANGHAI: TROOPS MARCH IN WHILE MEMBERS OF THE
CROWD HOLD PICTURE WITH CAPTION: "SUPPORT CHAIRMAN MAO, CONSTRUCT A NEW CHINA."

ABOVE: THE LIBERATION OF SHANGHAI: THE RADICAL TRAMWORKERS' UNION DECORATED THEIR VEHICLES TO WELCOME THE COMMUNISTS. THE LEGEND ON THE FRONT HERE READS: "CELEBRATE THE LIBERATION OF SHANGHAI."

OPPOSITE: THE LIBERATION OF SHANGHAI: ANOTHER SIGN AMONG THE CROWD. THIS ONE HAS WORKERS AND PEASANTS DESTROYING IMPERIALISM, FEUDALISM, AND BUREAUCRATIC CAPITALISM.

ON OCTOBER 1, 1949, MAO ANNOUNCED THE FORMAL ESTABLISHMENT OF THE PEOPLE'S REPUBLIC OF CHINA.

1949–1960

PLAIN LIVING AND HARD STRUGGLE

Life improved with victory. Mao, now 56, moved into a home in the Forbidden City, the center of Beijing, formerly forbidden to the common people. Like many Chinese houses, Mao's home had a high wall surrounding a small courtyard in which were planted trees and flowers. The house itself was more like a bungalow, sparsely furnished with chairs, sofas, bookshelves, and a worktable. There Mao entertained guests, played cards with visitors, and spent his free days with his wife and children. The life was simple and very private.

Even in public, people noted the simplicity of his habits. His meals were virtually spartan: some soup, soy noodles with bits of beef and peppers (still his favorite food), and fried vegetables. He drank plain water. And he continued to smoke heavily until his final years when doctors ordered him to cut back.

His hobby, if it can be called that, was swimming. He had been fond of it in his youth, but the harsh conditions in the Soviet areas seldom allowed him the time or opportunity to swim. In Beijing he had a pool built by his house and took up swimming with a passion. By 1956, when he was 62, he had so mastered the sport that he could swim across the broad Yangzi river three times. Exhilarated by the feat, he wrote these lines:

"I swim across the ten-thousand-*li* long Yangzi....
  I don't care about the blowing of the wind
    or the beating of the waves;
  It beats strolling in a quiet courtyard."

His work varied according to the needs of the moment. As the grand statesman and symbol of China, he regularly participated in social events, such as the welcoming of ambassadors and foreign visitors. This usually entailed entertaining in the nearby National Assembly building and posing for the customary group picture. With special guests and personal friends, such as Edgar Snow, he entertained at home, talking late into the night and then seeing his guest to the door. Like an ordinary host, he would stand outside, waving, until the guest drove off and then return into the house.

In keeping with his mass-line style of leadership, he made a yearly tour of the provinces to check on conditions and keep in touch with the masses. He visited factories and farms, and discussed the details of everyday life. This investigation of local conditions, which made him famous in the 1920s, continued right up until 1971, when increasingly bad health prevented it.

Mao's simple, vigorous life was his way of continuing the revolution, in keeping with a strategy worked out in 1949:

"If our forefathers, and we also, could weather long years of extreme difficulty and defeat powerful domestic and foreign reactionaries, why can't we now, after victory, build a prosperous and flourishing country? As long as we keep to our style of plain living and hard struggle, as long as we stand united, and as long as we persist in the people's democratic dictatorship and unite with our foreign friends, we shall be able to win speedy victory on the economic front."

The austere life-style suited Mao and the requirements of guerrilla war. But problems would arise in applying it to a vast country at peace.

LEANING TO ONE SIDE

During World War II, when the United States and the Soviet Union were allies, Mao sought support from both, especially the United States, since it had the most to give. As the Cold War began, Mao came out firmly on the side of the Soviet Union. He justified his policy with the example of Sun Yatsen:

"The forty years' experience of Sun Yatsen and the 28 years' experience of the Communist party have taught us to lean to one side....Throughout his life, Sun Yatsen appealed countless times to the capitalist countries for help and got nothing but heartless rebuffs. Only once in his whole life did Sun Yatsen receive foreign help, and that was Soviet help."

Following the example of Sun, Mao turned to the Soviet Union for help. In December 1949 he made his first trip abroad, to Moscow, to negotiate a treaty to replace the one which the Soviet Union had signed with Chiang Kaishek in 1945.

The negotiation process was not easy. It took more than two months, although Mao came with the expectation that it would take only a few weeks.

IN THE SOVIET UNION, MAO VISITED COLLECTIVE FARMS. HERE HE IS RECEIVING A REPORT ON THE "LUCH" COLLECTIVE NEAR MOSCOW.

IN THE SOVIET UNION, MAO VISITED COLLECTIVE FARMS. HERE HE TOURS A HOTHOUSE UNDER CONSTRUCTION.

Apparently the stumbling block was Soviet mistrust of China's friendship. Chiang Kaishek had once claimed to be a revolutionary and close friend of the Soviet Union; yet after he used the Soviet aid for his own purposes, he betrayed them. More recently, in June 1948, Stalin broke with Tito, the independent Yugoslavian Communist leader unwilling to accept Stalin's commands. Stalin suspected Mao might be "another Tito," who would turn out to be an enemy instead of a friend.

To mollify Stalin, Mao and the rest of the Chinese delegation launched a campaign to convince him of Mao's friendship. Ten-year-old speeches in praise of Stalin were supplied to the Soviet press. Mao dutifully made the rounds at Soviet model factories and collective farms, praising them as "models for construction in New China." Finally, before he left Moscow, Mao declared, "The friendship between China and the Soviet Union is eternal and indestructible." Apparently Stalin still wasn't totally convinced, but he did agree to significant concessions.

The thirty-year Treaty of Friendship, Alliance, and Mutual Assistance abrogated the 1945 treaty with Chiang's government and established a new Sino-Soviet alliance. Some $300 million in loans were provided to China over a five-year period. Outer Mongolia was made independent, while Inner Mongolia remained a part of China. The Soviet Union kept control, temporarily, of certain Manchurian railroads and ports. (By agreement they were to be returned in 1952, but they were not returned until after the Korean war in 1954.) These agreements, although inadequate for China's overall needs, did lay the basis for a decade of Sino-Soviet cooperation.

Sino-American relations meanwhile deteriorated. In the United States, the Truman administration came under attack for "losing China" and defended itself by denouncing the Communists with equal fervor. In China, Mao denied charges of "foreign domination" and used American governmental debates to expose the perfidy of imperialism.

Yet some glimmers of hope for improved relations remained. Secretary of State Acheson expressed willingness to "face the situation as it exists in fact." In August 1949 Mao wrote that "closest friendship" might be possible in the future. As late as January 1950, prospects for improved relations seemed even more favorable. Truman and Acheson both explicitly denied any intention of coming to the aid of Chiang Kaishek's new government on Taiwan, and the United Kingdom recognized the People's Republic.

In June all this was changed by the outbreak of hostilities in Korea. Though the Chinese were in no way involved in Korea, Truman immediately ordered the Seventh Fleet to go to the defense of Taiwan, thereby reversing the previous movement toward neutrality.

The Chinese did not want to enter the Korean war. Their main concern was Taiwan and their own unfinished civil war. During the first few months of fighting, they made vigorous protests, but remained uninvolved. American analysts took this to be a failure of will. Therefore in October, when Zhou Enlai, China's foreign minister, used the Indian ambassador to relay the urgent message that China would act if threatened, General MacArthur, the American field commander, dismissed the danger of direct Chinese involvement and moved his troops to the Chinese border. With their warnings disregarded by Washington and their crucial Manchurian industries threatened by the American advance, the Chinese reluctantly entered the war in October 1950.

Mao could not have been enthusiastic about the war, though foreign conflicts have often been used to win support for governments. First of all, it was not his kind of war. Chinese troops on foreign soil could not fight a true people's war, even if they had Korean support. Second, Mao was itching to begin agrarian reform at home. Two days before the shooting began in Korea, Mao announced: "The test of war is basically over.... Now it's the test of agrarian reform that we must pass." Third, he could not have appreciated the effect on Sino-American relations. The American war effort required propaganda which vilified the People's Republic and overturned Mao's own efforts to better relationships. Finally, the war meant a personal loss for Mao. His oldest son, Anying, the offspring of his marriage to Yang Kaihui, died in the fighting.

The war itself proved largely inconclusive. One year after its start, the fighting was stalemated where it began, along the 38th parallel; but it was

MAO ANYING (1921–1950), MAO'S SON WHO DIED IN
THE KOREAN WAR.

Agrarian reform began during the civil war,
when the extension of Communist power to an area
brought a "settling of accounts" and the redis-
tribution of land, which in turn usually produced
recruits for the Communists' cause. Yet the final
military victory in the civil war, so swift and
sweeping, left 80 percent of China's villages un-
touched by land reform. Landlords, only 4 percent
of the population, still owned 30 percent of the
land and wielded considerable power over the
peasants.

The new People's Republic passed generally
moderate legislation to eliminate the "idle rich"
gentry that made no contribution to production,
while reassuring well-to-do peasants who accounted
for half of China's agricultural production. Then
hysteria triggered by the Korean crisis torpedoed
the moderate policy. Landlords and their agents
expected the Americans or Chiang Kaishek to come
back and rescue them. The government became
frightened by thoughts of potential spies and sabo-
teurs. Poor peasants wronged in the past used this
climate to settle their grudges.

Mao later estimated that 750,000 people died in
the various campaigns against counterrevolution-
aries during these years. He remarked that he personally would have preferred that the policy of "no
executions and few arrests" had been carried out,
but the government had to allow the peasants to
settle their "blood debts" rather than protect the
landlords and possibly lose peasant support.

By 1952 land reform was completed. Landlords
no longer existed as a class. The most tyrannical
had been killed or sent to labor camps. The majority of the 18 million people in landlord families
were simply divested of their large holdings and
given a small plot to work like any other peasant.
The peasants thereby achieved a large degree of
democracy and prosperity; agricultural production
increased 15 percent each year and exceeded pre-
war levels.

Yet the problem of China's poverty remained.
Before the war China was the second poorest country in the world, with a per capita annual income of
$29 (as compared to $554 in Depression-ridden
America). No matter how equally China's wealth
was shared, the continued improvement of living

another two years before a formal truce ended the
last of the fighting.

The deadlock in Korea did have a positive effect
on one group. Chiang Kaishek's forces, saved
from final defeat by the American intervention,
regrouped and turned Taiwan into an impregnable
bastion from which they carried on a diplomatic
struggle designed to deprive the People's Republic
of the fruits of victory in the civil war. What the
Nationalists lost on the battlefield, they thereby
regained at the bargaining table. It would take the
People's Republic two decades of hard politicking
to overcome the diplomatic debacle, and during
that time improved relations with the United States
were impossible.

standards depended on industrialization and the mechanization of agriculture; otherwise China would always have too many people pressing on too little land. (As a comparison, China has 50 percent more people and 20 percent *less* arable land than India.)

The first five-year plan, begun in 1953, followed the Soviet model of funneling resources into the most productive sectors and concentrating power in the hands of a single manager. Everything was "scientifically" decided. And the results predictably followed in the Soviet's footsteps—steel production up 300 percent; coal, 100 percent; electricity, 166 percent; cement, 140 percent—during the five-year plan. Workers got higher wages. Students flocked to technical schools. But the peasants and the countryside lagged behind.

Mao was distressed by this aping of the Soviet Union which ignored China's own historical development, especially the experiences garnered in Yanan. Moreover, it sometimes led to ridiculous consequences. Later, Mao told a 1958 conference how this dogmatic copying of the Soviet Union affected him personally:

"I couldn't have eggs or chicken soup for three years because an article appeared in the Soviet Union which said that one shouldn't eat them. Later they said that one could eat them. It didn't matter if the article was correct or not, the Chinese listened all the same and respectfully obeyed. In short, the Soviet Union was tops."

But in the mid-1950s Mao did not voice such criticisms. In a July 1955 essay on agricultural cooperation, he wrote that the Soviet Union had faced developmental problems and solved them by the collectivization of agriculture, "and we can solve ours only by the same method." Yet in the same essay he articulated two principles which in effect reversed the previous Soviet-ordained priorities.

When he wrote that "socialist industrialization cannot be carried out in isolation from agricultural cooperation," he restored the importance which the countryside had lost in Soviet development. The thesis that "the technical transformation will take longer than the social" meant that cooperation need not wait upon the delivery of tractors (and thus the prior development of industry), as many Soviet economists believed.

In essence, Mao argued that production could be increased simply by people working together. Mechanization, to be sure, did accompany economies of scale (tractors are economical for large farms, but not for small gardens), but these economies did not have to await mechanization. If a group of farmers got together, they could dig an irrigation ditch to water their plots, rather than each carrying buckets of water to their individual plots.

Mao's points were not simply theoretical. He based his argument on Chinese experience, such as the struggle of the poor peasants of a village in Henan province who wanted to form a co-op in 1953. Richer peasants jeered, "They have less money than an egg has fur, and they think they can form a cooperative. Can a feather fly up to heaven?" The poor peasants succeeded, and two years later Mao reported, "The old system is dying, and a new system is being born. Chicken feathers really are flying up to heaven." The radicalism of the poor disproved the conservatism of the wealthy.

The activism of the masses encountered another problem: bureaucracy. Mao chastised the party cadre "tottering along like a woman with bound feet and constantly complaining, 'You're going too fast,' " and he added, "excessive criticism, inappropriate complaints, endless anxiety, and the erection of countless taboos—they believe this is the proper way to guide the socialist mass movement in the rural areas."

As a "cure" Mao suggested that they "spend some time going among the masses." A party in touch with the masses would share their enthusiasm, Mao thought. He was right. After his prodding, the party got behind the "socialist upsurge" in the countryside. Collectivization was rapidly completed.

By 1956, despite some problems, basic property relations changed, and China ceased to be a capitalist country. Just as land reform had brought private property to the peasants as individuals, collectivization created group property, still private in the legal sense, but shared by the people of one or more villages. In the cities, a similar process went on, as capitalists sold (and sometimes gave) their property to the state in return for a regular annuity. Those who ran their own businesses stayed on as the managers now paid by the state. Yet Mao warned that "although in the main socialist transformation has been completed with respect to the system of ownership, . . . the class struggle is by no means over. . . . In this respect the question of which will win out, socialism or capitalism, is still not really settled."

In the period of agrarian reform, a new Mao emerged. At the beginning he was still very much the guerrilla fighter who relied on land reform as an integral part of the people's war. By the end he was a political philosopher grappling practically with the question of socialist construction and bureaucracy in China. This question would dominate the last twenty years of his life.

LET A HUNDRED FLOWERS BLOOM

Mao now entered a period of vigorous intellectual effort. Whereas in 1955 he bemoaned the lack of experience and advocated "plunging into the struggles of the socialist revolution and learning in the process," by 1956 he was able to outline ten "problems" or "relationships" which posed a new course of development that would take advantage of China's being "poor" and "blank." In essence, Mao proposed balanced growth, in which all would share, rather than focused growth, which only benefited a few in the short run. This emphasis shifted from city to countryside, from heavy industry to light industry, and from the most advanced to the relatively backward.

The party showed no enthusiasm for Mao's new ideas. Liu Shaoqi, later Mao's nemesis in the Cultural Revolution, dismissed them with the remark: "What was done to win the revolutionary war cannot be applied to China's construction." Apathy was so great that Mao's ideas were not even published. The speech outlining the ten "relationships" was circulated only in the form of notes taken at the time.

Such indifference could exist because of the political bombshell exploded by Khrushchev at the Twentieth Congress of the Soviet Communist party in February 1956. To a select circle of Communist leaders, the Soviet party boss made a "secret speech" denouncing Stalin. The news soon leaked, and the belated admission of fallibility in the revolutionary ranks generated uncontrollable

shock waves. Mao described himself as being "very happy" when he heard the news, but also "apprehensive." His happiness stemmed from the inevitable loosening of the straitjacket of the Soviet model for development. His apprehension came because conservative bureaucrats could use Khrushchev's flaying of the "cult of personality" as an excuse to ignore Mao.

Despite a defense of Stalin by Mao, who argued that the late dictator should be seen in historical perspective, the Chinese Communist party was generally favorable to Khrushchev's ideas, especially his criticism of the cult of personality. The Eighth Party Congress, held seven months after that of the Soviets and controlled by Liu Shaoqi and Deng Xiaoping, therefore deleted "Mao Zedong thought" from the party's guiding principles and reduced Mao's power in the party by making Deng its general secretary. Subsequently Mao, now 63, retired as chairman of the government, and Liu replaced him, with the title of president.

Mao agreed to these changes. Ostensibly he was retiring to a second line of command, where he could focus his energies on broader questions rather than on day-to-day policy. Simultaneously he was grooming a new generation of revolutionary successors. In this way, at least theoretically, Mao could still deal with problems of development, and China would avoid a cataclysmic succession crisis. But Mao soon found that he was treated like a "dead ancestor," and that his longterm ideas were ignored. Frustrated by the party's response, he turned to a new forum to air his ideas.

Throughout 1956 the Communists had been concerned with winning over the old intelligentsia. Zhou Enlai believed they were necessary for socialist modernization. Mao was more interested in vigorous intellectual debate than in the intellectuals themselves. (Himself an intellectual, Mao nonetheless scorned other intellectuals' infatuation with useless knowledge.) Both Mao and Zhou promoted the Hundred Flowers campaign, which was to "let a hundred flowers bloom and a hundred schools of thought contend." Yet intellectuals responded very cautiously to this call to speak their minds. When they did get up the nerve to speak, party bureaucrats, nervous after the popular revolts in Hungary and Poland in the wake of Khrushchev's

RIGHT: KEEPING IN TOUCH WITH THE MASSES: MAO MEETS KURBAN TULUM, A PEASANT FROM THE UIGHUR NATIONAL MINORITY.

IN A LIGHTER MOMENT MAO CHARMS THE YOUNG WOMEN OF THE NEW DEMOCRATIC YOUTH LEAGUE IN 1957.

IN SICHUAN PROVINCE MAO VISITS THE HOME OF MRS. WEN.

speech, quickly discouraged them. The campaign was in danger of sputtering to a halt in February 1957, when Mao decided to give it a major push.

"On the Correct Handling of Contradictions Among the People" called for criticism of the Communist party; it was Mao's way of forcing the bureaucrats into motion by using the intellectuals. The full speech was not made public for four months, but certain ideas spread like wildfire through the intellectual community:

"If Marxism feared criticism, and if it could be overthrown by criticism, it would be worthless.... Fighting against wrong ideas is like being vaccinated—a person develops greater immunity from disease as the result of vaccination. Plants raised in a hothouse are unlikely to be sturdy."

"All attempts to use administrative orders or coercive measures to settle ideological questions or questions of right and wrong are not only ineffective but harmful."

The speech touched off several months of criticism aimed, for example, at "party members and cadres who wore worn-out shoes in the past, but now travel first-class and wear woolen uniforms." In the universities a political "storm" broke loose, with students occupying offices and holding party officials hostage.

The extreme tone of some of the criticisms shocked many party officials, who demanded and received the right to crack down on the most important dissidents. Mao, however, by this time had achieved his goal of shaking up the bureaucracy. The way was now paved for a "great leap forward."

THE GREAT LEAP FORWARD

The first five-year plan made great progress, which, unfortunately, still failed to meet China's tremendous needs. To remedy this problem, China's leaders planned an intensive production drive, similar to the one made by the Soviet Union in 1935, after its first five-year plan. The Soviet drive, symbolized by Alexei Stakhanov, a coalminer who produced fourteen times his usual amount in September 1935, stressed increased production within the established industrial and state structure. The Chinese drive, informed by Mao's vision, forged new structures, in particular, the people's commune.

In the beginning of the movement in early 1958, Mao merely outlined a theory of uninterrupted revolution and two methods of leadership:

"In making revolution one must strike while the iron is hot: one revolution must follow another; the revolution must continually advance. The Hunanese often say, 'Straw sandals have no pattern; they shape themselves in the making.' "

"There are two lines for building socialism: is it better to go about it coldly and deliberately, or boldly and joyfully?"

The Chinese people answered, "Boldly and joyfully." An extraordinary bountiful harvest in the spring of 1958 convinced them of the virtues of collective effort, and led many to predict that three years of struggle could lead to a "thousand years of Communist happiness."

Their optimism fed on the Soviet Union's success in putting into orbit the first man-made satellite, "Sputnik," an event that led Mao to proclaim, "The East wind prevails over the West wind," meaning that the socialist bloc had surpassed the capitalist countries.

The euphoria led to widespread recitation of Marx's description of Communist society, where one would be able to "hunt in the morning, fish in the afternoon, rear cattle in the evening, criticize after dinner, just as I have a mind, without ever becoming a hunter, fisher, shepherd, or critic." In largely rural China, where these were daily tasks, Marx's vision had a compelling and credible appeal.

From this ferment emerged the first commune, appropriately named "Sputnik." Peasants in Henan province carried the co-op movement one step farther, and merged "industry, agriculture, commerce, education, and the military into one big commune" which could take on the responsibilities of the state and thereby become the basic unit of society. Mao went to visit and liked what he saw: "If there is one commune like this, then there can be many of them." Within months 90 percent of peasant households adopted the communal form.

What Mao had seen was a recreation of the Yanan model of self-reliance. The Henan peasants introduced into their villages industries to produce needed organic fertilizer, mill their grain, and even make their clothes, thereby reducing dependence on the outside and breaking down the division of town and countryside.

As the movement gathered momentum, grander

RIGHT: IN HIS HOMETOWN OF SHAOSHAN, MAO
RELAXES WITH A LOCAL PEASANT FAMILY.

BELOW: IN ZHEJIANG, MAO INSPECTS THE
EXPERIMENTS OF AN AGRICULTURAL COLLEGE.

OPPOSITE PAGE: HERE HE CHECKS OUT THE
HENAN PROVINCE HARVEST FIRSTHAND.

goals were espoused. Communal kitchens and daycare centers were organized, to free women from the drudgery of housework and make them available for productive labor. Dams and irrigation canals were started, and often rapidly completed, in the first flush of collective effort. Even heavy industry came to the countryside, as commune after commune built "backyard" furnaces to forge iron and steel. National defense was to be taken over by the newly formed peasant militias.

But the spontaneous movement failed, perhaps of necessity, to follow any careful plan. Though the government issued a directive to limit communes to 2,000 families, in the fall of 1958 the average commune had 5,000 families. Often people were unclear on what exactly a commune was. A popular ditty went: A people's commune's great/ It really is just so.../ But what it actually is/ I don't even know. The sudden appearance of economic units ranging in size from 5,000 to 100,000 people was often too much for untutored peasant administrators.

By late 1958 the Leap Forward had reversed direction. Food shortages hit those communes where planting was neglected in the enthusiasm for public works. Resentment in varying degrees cropped up when the original expectations were not met—regardless of who was to blame. Most importantly, production, which the Great Leap was intended to promote, fell as the lack of planning and forethought manifested itself in supply shortages and bottlenecks.

Mao, still party chairman and the promoter of the Leap, came under attack from other party leaders. Peng Dehuai, the minister of defense, was particularly incensed by the deprofessionalization of the army just at the time the United States installed guided missiles on Taiwan and threatened to "unleash" Chiang Kaishek. After returning from a visit to the Soviet Union, Peng circulated a "letter of opinion" condemning "petty bourgeois fanaticism" (which Mao had criticized in 1953 as the source of "left opportunist" errors). At about the same time, Khrushchev in Poland denounced the communes and Chinese ideas of Communism. (He reportedly once described Chinese Communism as two peasants with one pair of pants.) Liu Shaoqi expressed serious reservations about "excessive" and "extreme" developments. Deng Xiaoping, in

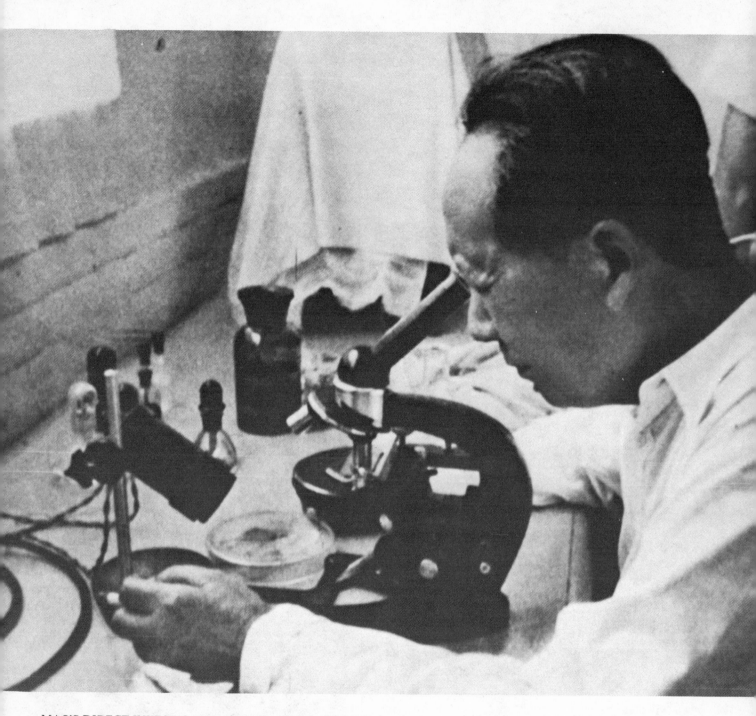

MAO'S DIRECT INVESTIGATION OF THE CONDITIONS IN THE COUNTRYSIDE LED HIM TO CALL FOR A GREAT LEAP FORWARD. HERE IN XUSHUI COUNTY HE EXAMINES THE PRODUCTION OF AN ORGANIC FERTILIZER PLANT AT ONE OF THE FIRST COMMUNES.

ALSO IN XUSHUI COUNTY HE SEES A PEASANT-RUN CLOTHING FACTORY IN OPERATION.

LEFT: MAO HIMSELF PARTICIPATED IN THE EXTRA WORK EFFORT. HERE HE HELPS BUILD A RESERVOIR OUTSIDE BEIJING IN 1958.

THE GREAT LEAP WAS FUNDAMENTALLY A MODERNIZATION DRIVE. ONE OF ITS LESSER–KNOWN ASPECTS WAS THE PRODUCTION OF MORE THAN 200 TYPES OF MOTOR VEHICLES, SOME OF WHICH ARE SEEN HERE PARADING THROUGH BEIJING. NOTE THE STYLISH WHITEWALL TIRES.

THE GREAT LEAP FORWARD WAS BASED ON PREVIOUSLY UNTAPPED LABOR. HERE PEASANTS WORK IN THE WINTER ON A WATER–CONSERVATION PROJECT.

TO MODERNIZE, CHINA NEEDED STEEL; SO PEASANTS SET OUT TO BUILD FURNACES.

OPPOSITE: THE FINAL PRODUCT, THE SO-CALLED BACKYARD FURNACES, WERE VERY EDUCATIONAL, BUT NOT ALWAYS VERY PRODUCTIVE.

THE INTEGRATION OF NATIONAL DEFENSE AND AGRICULTURE. PEASANT MILITIAMEN DRILLED IN THE FIELDS WHERE THEY WORKED.

PEASANT MILITIA ON THE MARCH.

COMMUNITY CANTEENS, ACCORDING TO THE WESTERN PRESS, WERE
INTENDED TO DESTROY THE FAMILY. HERE AT A COMMUNAL CANTEEN IN
XUSHUI COUNTY THREE GENERATIONS SIT DOWN TO EAT TOGETHER.

LEFT: PENG DEHUAI, THE CHIEF OPPONENT OF THE GREAT LEAP.

a scarcely veiled reference to going either "coldly and deliberately" or "boldly and joyfully," observed that "a donkey is certainly slow, but it rarely has an accident."

The final showdown came in August at Lushan, a popular mountain resort. The party's central committee, along with invited military and local officials, met to assess the damage of the Leap. For nearly three weeks criticisms were vented before Mao had the chance to speak.

When his turn at last came, he was a bit distraught. For three days he had gone without sleep, even after taking sleeping pills. But he was still anxious to explain his position. He accepted the blame for the worst problems, especially the backyard furnaces, which had come under the greatest attack. "The chaos was on a great scale," he said, "and I take responsibility." But he also argued that everyone makes mistakes, and he alone did not bear responsibility. Then he played his trump card. he asked the party to choose between him and Peng

Dehui, and threatened, if the communes were allowed to fail, to "go the the countryside and lead the peasants against the government."

The party decided in favor of Mao. The Great Leap and the communes were reaffirmed. Peng Dehuai, accused of collusion with the Soviet Union because his criticisms were similar to those of Khrushchev, was ousted and replaced as head of the army by Lin Biao, a hero of the civil war and a disciple of Mao's military ideas.

But bad weather and continued Soviet opposition conspired to prevent any revival of the Great Leap. Several years of drought brought smaller crops, which the peasants, more familiar with scarcity than plenty, had little enthusiasm to share. Khrushchev, confronted with the anomaly of Soviet experts helping to construct projects which the Soviet Union opposed, finally withdrew them in August 1960. Their sudden departure dashed any remaining hopes for rapid economic progress. A period of retrenchment began.

IN 1957 MAO VISITED THE SOVIET UNION AND TOLD CHINESE STUDENTS THERE THAT "THE SOCIALIST CAMP MUST HAVE A LEADER AND THAT LEADER IS THE SOVIET UNION."

THE SMILES FOR THE CAMERAS BELIED THE TENSIONS UNDERLYING THE MEETING OF MAO AND
KHRUSHCHEV IN AUGUST 1958.

MAO, KHRUSCHCHEV, AND LIU SHAOQI IN BEIJING, OCTOBER 1959, SOON AFTER SINO–SOVIET HOSTILITIES WERE MADE PUBLIC.

1960–1976

MAO AT LUSHAN, A MOUNTAIN RESORT, IN 1961. AT THIS TIME THE WESTERN PRESS CLAIMED HIS HEALTH WAS FAILING.

CALM BEFORE THE STORM

The tumultuous 1960s began quietly for Mao. His bold leadership style did not serve the needs of a China trying to recover from economic losses suffered during the Great Leap Forward. He was out of touch with the daily affairs in the party and the government. Even his public ceremonial appearances became more and more infrequent.

Mao's low public profile fed rumors in the West. The *New York Times* of May 27, 1962, reported: "Mao...is known to be in failing health with his mental powers faltering. There are surely cleavages in the Chinese Communist leadership as between the moderates and the extremists that could burst into a struggle for control when Mao dies." (In fact, the struggle would come because Mao lived.)

Though beginning to feel his seventy years and tiring a bit sooner than in his youth, Mao was neither sick nor senile, and still a very vigorous man. By all accounts, he still maintained his simple life and habits with his wife and their two daughters in Beijing.

In January of 1962, Mao made a brief return to the political stage to deliver a speech to 7,000 local party leaders. His message was simple: "In our work of socialist construction, we are still to a very large extent working blindly....We must put in a lot of hard work and make thorough investigations." The revolution could not go forward unless the party maintained its close ties with the masses. If it did not go forward, Mao predicted, "the dictatorship of the proletariat will be transformed into a bourgeois dictatorship, into a reactionary fascist dictatorship."

Mao also gave a more personal warning to the party bureaucrats: "Those of you who shirk responsibility, who do not allow people to speak, who think you are tigers, and that nobody will dare to touch your ass, whoever has this attitude, ten out of ten of you will fail. People will talk anyway. You think that nobody will really dare to touch the ass of tigers like you? They damn well will!"

These warnings were repeated in September; both times they were ignored. A few words from Mao were not enough to stop the widespread demoralization and corruption of cadres as the revolution slipped backward instead of going forward. Government policies to increase production at any cost were playing into the hands of rich peasants, who started by making extra money legally in the "free" markets outside state control and soon moved to bribing officials to bend the rules in their favor. People lost faith in revolutionary change; some even reverted to old superstitions and magic. A decade of revolutionary rule weighed lightly in the balance against two millennia of feudal dynasties.

In January 1963, Mao returned to the fray, declaring this intention in a poem:

> "So many deeds cry out to be done,
> And always urgently;
> The world rolls on, time presses.
> Ten thousand years are too long.
> Seize the day, seize the hour!"

The criticisms that he made in 1962 were now formulated into a directive, known as the "First Ten Points," that laid the foundation for a new movement, the Socialist Education Movement, which was to concern itself with the decline of cooperation and the rise of corruption in the countryside. Mao used the Ten Points to hammer home once again his message of the importance of social practice and investigation for knowledge:

"Where do correct ideas come from? Do they drop from the skies? No. Are they innate in the mind? No. They come from social practice and it alone; they come from three kinds of social practice: the struggle for production, the class struggle, and scientific experiment."

From this analysis, Mao concluded that the correct way to handle rural corruption was to rely on the poor and "lower-middle" peasants. At issue was a class struggle, and they were the natural recruits for a revolutionary class army. To be without them was "like a commander without troops, whose words fall on deaf ears, and who is without help in doing anything and unable to move even an inch." On the other hand, with them, Mao said, "Once class struggle is grasped, miracles are possible."

But Mao's idea of party reform from the bottom was not shared by the top party leaders, who preferred reform from the top. Deng Xiaoping, the party's general secretary, issued his own "Later Ten Points," and Liu Shaoqi, the head of govern-

IN 1963 MAO'S WIFE, JIANG QING, SUDDENLY REAPPEARED IN PUBLIC AFTER A QUARTER CENTURY IN OBSCURITY. HERE SHE (IN THE CENTER) AND MAO GREET MME SUKHARNO AT THE BEIJING AIRPORT.

MAO GREETING THE INDONESIAN PRESIDENT, SUKHARNO, IN 1961. INDONESIA AT THAT TIME WAS ONE OF CHINA'S MAIN ALLIES.

ment, followed with his "Revised Later Ten Points." In essence, these revisions of Mao shifted the movement from a class struggle based on the mobilized peasants to a simple party purge carried out by central officials. Liu insisted that "to launch the Socialist Education Movement at any point requires the sending of a work team from the higher level. The whole movement should be led by the work team." These work teams corrected the worst abuses, but prevented any thoroughgoing movement. The Socialist Education Movement brought no miracles.

THE SINO-SOVIET SPLIT

Sino-Soviet relations had always followed a bumpy, torturous road. Under Stalin the Soviet Union recognized the official government, while the Soviet Communist party maintained ties with the Chinese Communist party. The two relationships seldom meshed very well. After 1949 this problem was ameliorated but not removed. The Chinese Communists shared certain national interests with the previous government; so such issues as the control of the railways passing through Manchuria and the precise delineation of border lines remained matters of contention.

During the 1950s American hostility to both Communist powers forced them to paper over any differences. But they were there. After his 1954 visit to China, Khrushchev reportedly told his friends that Mao was very charming and gracious as they lounged around his pool; yet Khrushchev felt ill at ease. Conflict with China is inevitable, he told his listeners. Consequently Khrushchev always tried to keep his Chinese allies on a short leash. He mistrusted their intentions. When Mao refused to submit to nuclear blackmail, Khrushchev called him "bellicose" and suggested he see a psychiatrist. During the Taiwan straits crisis of 1958, Mao and Khrushchev again clashed, this time over tactics in dealing with America and the knotty problem of Chiang Kaishek. Hard feelings were exacerbated by Khrushchev's disapproval of the commune movement and his support for Peng Dehuai's attacks on the Great Leap Forward.

Somewhere around 1960 the alliance began to collapse. Perhaps it was the 1959 Camp David summit which warmed Soviet-American relations while frosting Sino-Soviet ties. Then again, the August 1960 withdrawal of Soviet technical experts, an effort by Khrushchev to put economic pressure on China, is often described as the straw that broke the camel's back. Certainly relations only worsened afterward. When the Russians joined with the Americans and British in a partial nuclear test ban treaty in 1963, the Chinese press accused the Soviets of entering into an anti-Chinese conspiracy.

Despite Chinese charges, Khrushchev's relations with the United States were not harmonious. The Cuban missile crisis of 1962, brought on by the placement of Soviet missiles in Cuba, nearly led to nuclear war, and indicated that tensions between Russians and Americans could still reach flash point. The war in Vietnam similarly reminded world opinion of the fragile foundation of detente. Were the Sino-Soviet split solely dictated by hostility to the United States, it could not have been so deep and unremitting.

The more important doctrinal root of the split lay in Mao's critique of "revisionism." Historically, revisionism refers to the right wing of the Communist movement, people who revised Marx's revolutionary message until it was reduced to simple reformism. Mao made such criticisms of the Soviet Union. As he watched the Chinese revolution develop and studied Soviet textbooks on how revolutions should develop, he concluded that the textbooks placed too much emphasis on material incentives and individualism, rather than on "politics in command" and "the mass line." Mao came to criticize Stalin, whose "basic error," in Mao's opinion, was "his distrust of the people." All this sharply contrasted with 1955, when Mao claimed, "The road traveled by the Soviet Union is our model."

Mao's critique of revisionism, once started, rapidly brought him to extremely radical conclusions. According to him, "The rise to power of revisionism means the rise to power of the bourgeoisie." In effect this meant a counterrevolution, described by Mao in a May 1964 talk as fascist in nature: "The Soviet Union today is under the dictatorship of the bourgeoisie, a dictatorship of the big bourgeoisie, a dictatorship of the German fascist type, a dictatorship of the Hitler type."

Yet, it must be noted, Mao's theories had confusing consequences. When Khrushchev was involuntarily retired in October 1964, partly for his handling of the Cuban missile crisis, and replaced by his former close associates, Brezhnev and Kosygin, Mao apparently thought this was the end of revisionism. He sent a letter to the new Russian leaders congratulating them on "the downfall of a buffoon." Mao seemed to suggest thereby that revisionism was a policy option easily changed, rather than a structural form of class rule. Could it be so easily changed? This question was made moot when relations with the new Russian rulers fared no better than those with Khrushchev. But the concept remained problematic, especially when it was applied to China.

GIRDING FOR STRUGGLE

The year 1965 dawned with Mao a bit tired and introspective. China had scored some victories: an atom bomb was exploded the previous October, and some crucial Third World countries, in particular Sukharno's Indonesia, had become allies. Perhaps China could survive without Soviet support. However, the United States was expanding its war in Vietnam, and many feared a repeat there of the war in Korea. In China itself, Mao was unhappy about the failure of the Socialist Education Movement to get off the ground.

One evening in January, Mao had dinner with his old friend, the American journalist Edgar Snow, and discussed these matters. He told Snow he thought war would be avoided, and expressed his "personal regret" that the "forces of history have divided and separated the American and Chinese people from virtually all communication during the past fifteen years." In discussing the Third World, he noted, "where severe oppression existed, there would be revolution."

Late that evening, Mao reminisced about his own life, about how many of his family and friends had been killed in the revolution, but he had always been spared, and about how he had started out to be a teacher, but wound up being a Communist. He told Snow he "was getting ready to see God very soon" and the revolution would have to be turned over to the youth, who would judge events by their own values. He closed by observing that the only

thing certain was change. A thousand years from now all of them, he said, including Marx, Engels, and Lenin, would possibly appear rather ridiculous.

Snow described their parting: "As the car drove away, I looked back and watched Mao brace his shoulders and slowly retrace his steps, leaning heavily on the arm of an aide, into the Great Hall of the People."

Yet even as his physical power waned, Mao was girding for his last struggle.

While the party ignored him, the army responded. The head of the army, Lin Biao, a short, spare, balding man who replaced the pugnacious Peng Dehuai in 1959, had been gradually reorganizing the army to eliminate the hierarchical structure of the 1950s and restore the old egalitarian form of the 1930s and 1940s. In doing so, Lin reintroduced intensive political study, for which he directed the compilation of key quotes from the writings of Mao. The final product came out in a convenient booklet format with a durable red plastic cover. Thus in May 1964, with Lin's imprimatur, the army published one of the cornerstones of the Cultural Revolution, *The Quotations of Chairman Mao Zedong,* better known as the "Little Red Book."

While the army studied the Red Book, Mao renewed pressure on the party for a movement from the bottom up. In phrases echoing the Great Leap Forward, Mao insisted. "We must boldly unleash the masses; we must not be like women with bound feet." Spoken less than a week after the conversation with Snow, these were the words of a man not yet ready to die.

THE CULTURAL REVOLUTION

The "Great Proletarian Cultural Revolution," begun in 1966, continued for ten years, until Mao died. Its repercussions were felt around the world and throughout Chinese society. Its meaning has been as diverse as the people it has touched. Perhaps its essence was captured by a remark Mao made to Andre Malraux, the French minister of culture:

"What is expressed by that commonplace term 'revisionism' is the death of the revolution. What we have just done in the army must be done every-

IN 1960 MIKOYAN, LIU SHAOQI, KHRUSHCHEV, AND DENG XIAOPING POSED TO DEMONSTRATE THEIR "CLOSEST UNITY." IN THE CULTURAL REVOLUTION, MAO ACCUSED LIU AND DENG OF ADHERING TO SOVIET–STYLE POLITICS AND LABELED LIU "CHINA'S KHRUSHCHEV."

where. I have told you revolution is also a feeling. If we decide to make of it what the Russians are now doing—a feeling of the past—everything will fall apart. Our revolution cannot be simply the stabilization of victory.''

The feeling of self-sacrifice, of serving the people, which forms the core of any ethical culture, had to be kept alive for the revolution to go forward. Yet, as Mao told Malraux, ''People do not like to bear the burden of revolution throughout their lives.'' Once victorious, they settle down to bureaucratic jobs, forget why they fought, and often become corrupt. They become ''women with bound feet,'' refusing to move forward.

If the original revolutionaries grew tired and lazy, what about the young who had never had to struggle? Mao saw in his nephew, the son of Zemin, a love of comfort and a fear of difficulties when the boy stayed in a warm swimming pool to avoid the cold surrounding air. Mao, the perennial physi-

cal culturalist unsoftened by time, chastised the boy and compared him unfavorably to his father. ''You grew up eating honey, and thus far you have never known suffering. . . . How can you be a leftist?'' If he thought this of his own nephew, what did he think of the rest of China's youth? Nevertheless Mao would turn to the youth, perhaps hoping that they would be steeled and tempered in the struggle.

The Cultural Revolution grew out of the Socialist Education Movement. It began when a Shanghai critic, Yao Wenyuan, blasted a popular play written by Wu Han, a vice-mayor of Beijing. The drama, set in the sixteenth century, concerned a just official dismissed from office by a tyrannical emperor. The play originally opened in 1960, in a political climate critical of Mao's handling of the Great Leap. The politically sophisticated knew that the just official represented Peng Dehuai, who had opposed Mao; by extension, Mao was portrayed as the vicious emperor. In 1965 Mao attempted, by means of Yao's article, to call a halt to this veiled political criticism. But Peng Zhen, the mayor of Beijing and head of the party's "Five-Person Group" for handling the revolutionization of culture, stifled the criticism. Mao was not being attacked merely by lesser party figures; the party's top echelon was blocking his moves.

Not one to flee from a fight, Mao launched a campaign against Wu Han from outside Beijing. He gathered radical critics and writers in Shanghai to keep up the attack on the play. Next he pulled in the army, still under the command of Lin Biao, Peng Dehuai's successor. Lin Biao and Mao's wife, Jiang Qing, held a forum on literature and art, and then used army cultural groups to disseminate the forum's pro-Mao conclusions. Denunciations of the "black line" quickly spread through the land. Wu Han quickly fell, while Peng Zhen and several other Beijing officials were compromised by their defense of him. The criticism drummed on until May, when Peng Zhen was dismissed from office, actually "locked out" by insubordinate employees.

Mao was not content with his victory over Peng Zhen. The experience of early 1966 convinced him that a large-scale movement was necessary. At a May 1966 meeting of the party's central committee, he argued not only that Peng Zhen should be denounced, but that all the "capitalist roaders" be searched out and expelled. Such "ghosts and monsters" could only be discovered by a full-scale cultural revolution. The central committee agreed with Mao, and issued a circular to this effect on May 16. Those opposed to him no doubt thought it would be easier to sabotage the movement than to confront Mao directly.

The May call to "thoroughly expose the reactionary bourgeois stand of so-called academic authorities" provoked an explosion on the campus of Beijing University. A young philosophy instructor pasted up a "big-character poster" or wall newspaper bitterly condemning the school president. After Mao praised this poster, students everywhere followed suit. Soon no academic authority could escape a withering barrage of revolutionary rhetoric. Officials suspected of impeding the revolutionization of China's culture were labeled "monsters and demons" and "counterrevolutionary re-

visionists of the Krushchev type."

But the party elite, following methods used to control the Socialist Education Movement, sent out work teams to direct and control the burgeoning revolution. They succeeded in restricting the student tempest to the academic teapot.

Mao retreated from Beijing once again. This time he headed south to Wuhan, where he swam the Yangzi river as he had in 1956, this time covering nearly ten miles in 65 minutes. (This seemingly incredible feat by a 72-year-old man becomes more comprehensible when we realize that the strong current carried him downstream and across; all Mao had to do was stay afloat.) The swim was Mao's way of declaring to the world that he was fit and ready for struggle.

He returned to Beijing immediately afterward, and called another meeting of the central committee. He expressed his distress at the suppression of the students. "It won't do just to sit in an office and listen to reports," he told them. "We should rely on and have faith in the masses, and make trouble to the end.... A life of sitting on the sofa in front of an electric fan won't do."

Two weeks later, Mao wrote his own big-character poster, entitled "Bombard the Headquarters." In it he accused "leading comrades" of enforcing "a bourgeois dictatorship" and imposing "a white terror." The charges, clearly aimed at Liu Shaoqi and Deng Xiaoping, immediately reduced their political influence. Mao held an effective majority in party councils, and further strengthened it by having his opponents downgraded.

Liu and Deng, formerly among the top handful of China's politicians, disappeared from public view in August 1966. As the public campaign against them heated up, they were put under house arrest, possibly for their own protection. Liu refused to recant and died a natural death while still in custody. Deng made a self-criticism and was rehabilitated politically in 1973. A major figure in China today, Deng outlived the forces who replaced him in 1966, the Red Guards.

THE RED GUARDS

High above on a parapet, the bronzed and belligerent Mao Zedong reviewed his troops. In the pounding heat of the mid-August sun, he held up

MAO DURING HIS SWIM. THE PICTURE SUGGESTS THAT MAO COVERED THE DISTANCE BY KEEPING HIS HEAD ABOVE WATER AND LETTING THE RIVER'S CURRENT PULL HIM ALONG.

OPPOSITE: MAO ABOARD SHIP ON THE DAY OF HIS FAMOUS SWIM ACROSS THE YANGZI RIVER.

MAO JOINS THE RED GUARDS.

his arm in greeting to the vast anarchic army of student activists known as the Red Guards. Only infrequently did he dip back into the building behind him to shed his jacket and wipe off the sweat streaming down his body. Millions of Red Guards had journeyed to Beijing to see him, if only from a distance, and he could not disappoint them.

Mao's idea at this point was fatally simple. The students, who were already spontaneously organizing themselves in response to his calls, could kill two birds with one stone. They could provide the mass force necessary to shake up Chinese society and purge it of old ideas; their youth made them a natural antidote to the false wisdom of age. At the same time they would gain the experience necessary to groom them as revolutionary successors. Uncorrupted by the old society, they were the natural leaders of the new one. As he told Chinese students in Moscow in 1957, "The world is yours as well as ours, but in the last analysis it is yours. You young people, full of vigor and vitality, are in the bloom of life, like the sun at eight or nine in the morning. Our hope is placed on you."

So, with Mao presiding, millions of students flocked to Beijing to "exchange experiences." The experiences were often minimal, and sometimes counterproductive. Students changed the names of streets, closed down religious shrines, assaulted "reactionaries" who favored Western ways or in some way or another displeased the youthful rebels. The majority did not engage in vandalism or violence. They used the unprecedented opportunity of free travel to engage in "revolutionary tourism" and see their own vast country firsthand. This phase of the movement climaxed in October. The strain on the economy proved too much for anxious officials, and Mao agreed with them that the students should be encouraged to stay home.

In late October Mao admitted to other leaders that so far the Cultural Revolution had "wreaked havoc," and he accepted responsibility for the confusion: "I myself had not foreseen that as soon as the Beijing University poster was broadcast, the whole country would be thrown into turmoil. Even before the letter to the Red Guards had gone out, Red Guards had mobilized throughout the country, and in one rush they swept you off your feet. Since

IN AUGUST 1966 A MILLION RED GUARDS MARCHED BEFORE MAO.

The Red Guards 153

it was I who caused the havoc, it is understandable that you have some bitter words for me."

Mao was not yet calling the revolution off or even toning it down. "It has only been five months. Perhaps the movement may last another five months, or even longer." Mao was willing to give it that time.

FACTIONALISM UNFETTERED

Mao's original plan attacked revisionism rather than revisionists, or the bureaucratic work style rather than individual bureaucrats. His earliest directives emphasized that 95 percent of cadres sided with the people. The remaining 5 percent consisted mostly of people whose hearts were in the right place, but who had lagged behind or made mistakes. Only a "handful" formed the hard-core opposition, "those who have wormed their way into the party and are taking the capitalist road." When discovered, these few were to be dismissed from their posts and replaced by revolutionaries.

The Cultural Revolution, truly revolutionary in its impact, went beyond Mao's original intent and provoked massive and often violent confrontations. In Shanghai, the "Workers' Rebel Headquarters," fifty to sixty thousand strong, clashed with the equally large "Workers' Red Militia Detachment." In Beijing, ex-soldiers, calling themselves the "Red Flag Army," used bricks and iron bars to break into state offices and demand settlement of their grievances. In Guangzhou, the "Rebel Red Guards" faced off against the "Red Flag Workers' Headquarters"; offices were raided, captives were taken, and these unfortunates were then led about the street. The struggle against bureaucratism in the name of Chairman Mao in many cases degenerated into unfettered factionalism which lost sight of the original goals.

In February 1967, Mao called two of the leading Shanghai leftists, Zhang Chunchiao and Yao Wenyuan, to Beijing to demand a halt to revolutionary excesses. He told them, "The slogan of 'Doubt everything and overthrow everything' is reactionary." Various structural changes, such as the elimination of titles, were similarly labeled. Students came in for criticism: "Our method of struggle should now be on a higher level. We

shouldn't keep on saying, 'Smash their dogs' head, down with so-and-so.' I think that university students should make a deeper study of things, and choose a few passages to write some critical articles about."

To help this process, the army was to participate in a "triple alliance" of soldiers, revolutionary cadre, and revolutionary masses which would forge new, unified "revolutionary committees" to replace the previous bureaucratic structure and end factionalism.

For Mao the task was simple; he wrote Lin Biao, the head of the army, "You should send the army to support the broad masses of the left." But identifying the "left" was not so simple when everyone claimed to be a leftist and the true follower of Mao. Moreover the army, despite reorganization and years of indoctrination, was no more immune to factionalism than the rest of the country.

In the central Chinese city of Wuhan, the army commander, General Chen Zaidao, supported a faction known as the "One Million Heroic Troops" which was besieging their opposition, the "Wuhan Workers' General Headquarters." Mao sent personal delegates from Beijing to Wuhan to order Chen to lift the siege. Chen, instead, arrested the delegates. This unprecedented crisis was not resolved until superior units were sent in, and Chen, confronted with military defeat, capitulated. This Wuhan "mutiny" revealed that the Cultural Revolution could pour over into real civil war.

Mao hastily made a secret visit to Wuhan to investigate the damage wrought by factionalism. He saw the destruction caused by the fighting between the two mass organizations and heard of the dead and the wounded. His observations convinced him that the revolution had gone too far and had to be brought back on course. When he returned to Beijing, he ordered the army to be brought under tighter control and then issued an instruction, signed by himself and all the other top leaders, that order was to be restored under the army's direction. The Communist party, paralyzed by the revolution, was to be rebuilt.

The emphasis on order by the man who said, "Make trouble to the end," marked a turn to the right. But Mao refused to see himself as anything but a man of the left. For him, continued revolutionary excesses while China tried to reunify could

MAO AND HIS "CLOSE COMRADE-IN-ARMS," LIN BIAO.

IN SHANGHAI NEARLY A MILLION STUDENTS DEMONSTRATED IN SUPPORT OF VIETNAM.

THE CULT OF MAO: IN 1965 THIS PLAY DRAMATIZED THE STRUGGLE TO TAME THE HUAI RIVER. IN THE BACKGROUND MAO'S CALLIGRAPHY READS: "THE HAI RIVER MUST BE BROUGHT UNDER PERMANENT CONTROL."

THE CULT OF MAO: A 1966 PLAY ABOUT THE LONG MARCH ENDED WITH MAO'S FACE APPEARING AS A RED SUN.

THE CULT OF MAO: IN 1965 THIS CARD SHOW AT AN ATHLETIC EVENT WAS ENTITLED "SUNFLOWERS FACE THE SUN."

ABOVE: THE CULT OF MAO: IN FACTORIES NO MACHINE COULD GO WITHOUT A PHOTO OF MAO.

OPPOSITE: THE CULT OF MAO: ON THE RIVERS BOATS BROUGHT IN THE BANANA HARVEST, ALONG WITH A SUITABLE PICTURE AND QUOTE FROM MAO.

THE CULT OF MAO: WHEN RADICALS TOOK OVER SHANGHAI IN 1967, ONE OF THEIR FIRST ACTS WAS TO PRODUCE AN OVERSIZED PORTRAIT OF MAO.

THE 1969 CELEBRATIONS FOR THE NINTH PARTY CONGRESS MARKED THE HEIGHT OF THE MAO CULT.

no longer be permitted; they constituted acts of counterrevolutionary "ultraleftism." Mao, now in the center beween the ultraleft and the right, joked that his position was "center-left."

It took two years for order to be restored. Not until April 1969 could a Communist party congress be held. Mao declared it, the ninth party congress and the first since 1958, "a congress of unity and a congress of victory." He also told the assembled party members that "the revolution has not been completed."

THE LIN BIAO AFFAIR

Mao was now 75 years old, and in failing health. He provided for his death by naming Lin Biao, the head of the army, as his successor. The choice was appropriate, since the reconstituted Communist party contained a high proportion of military men; 40 percent of the 1969 central committee held military posts. It looked as if Mao could quietly retire.

To Mao's surprise, his loyal successor and "close

comrade-in-arms" came out in opposition to him the following year. In a party meeting at the Lushan mountain retreat, Lin Biao, like the previous head of the army, Peng Dehuai, clashed with Mao over the direction of the revolution. However, whereas Peng had taken a position to Mao's right, Lin stood firmly to the left, in opposition not only to the restoration of bureaucrats criticized during the Cultural Revolution, but also to the latest foreign-policy initiative, rapprochement with the United States.

Mao responded with guerrilla tactics which he described as "throwing stones, mixing sand into soil, and undermining the wall." Translated, that meant he carried out a campaign of indirect criticism and political reorganization to weaken Lin's position, and in the fall of 1971 made one last provincial tour to garner support.

Lin Biao, realizing what Mao was doing, instigated a left-wing plot organized by his son, an air-force officer. Mao, described in the secret plans as "B-52," would be either assassinated or held under house arrest. The plot was discovered before it could be put into effect. When news of this

BY 1970 MAO WAS BEGINNING TO FAIL IN HEALTH AND TO COME UNDER ATTACK FROM HIS FORMER
ALLIES.

FEBRUARY 1972 MAO GREETS PRESIDENT NIXON.

reached Lin, he made a daring escape; by force and bluff he succeeded in boarding a plane to escape to the Soviet Union. However, the plane crashed under mysterious circumstances in Outer Mongolia, and Lin is presumed to have gone down with the plane.

THE NIXON VISIT

The arrival of an American president with great pomp and ceremony in Beijing signaled the final master stroke in Mao's long political career. His concern with revisionism and Soviet hegemony in China had driven him inexorably toward a rupture of that uneasy alliance. By 1969 the verbal hostility had even precipitated a border conflict, in which Chinese and Soviet lives were lost. Mao considered this the final dissolution of the socialist bloc. To analyze this political conjuncture, Mao developed his last political theory, that of the "three worlds."

Mao's theory of the three worlds subtly reordered the older concept, in which the community of nations was divided into the industrial democracies, the socialist bloc, and the "Third World" or developing nations. Whereas the last group remained as it was, the "first" world became the two "superpowers," the United States and the Soviet Union, and the "second" world was occupied by "intermediate" nations, largely those of Eastern and Western Europe. The value of this theory for China lay in its focus on the superpowers as the main source of international tension; and attention could be further narrowed to one or the other superpower. Meanwhile, denial of any obligation for socialist solidarity allowed improved relations with all other countries; China did not have to link itself solely with the Third World or either of the major blocs.

Like his other notions, this idea of Mao's was not readily accepted. Lin Biao, for one, had strong reservations against improved relations with the United States, and this apparently was a factor in his coup attempt. But Mao had strong support from Zhou Enlai, who handled the top-secret negotiations with Henry Kissinger that finally made the Nixon visit possible.

The bold strokes were Mao's own. It was he who decided to circumvent customary diplomatic channels by tendering an invitation to President Nixon through Edgar Snow and the pages of *Life* magazine. In a December 1970 interview with Snow, Mao made the astounding remark that Nixon would be welcome "either as a tourist or as President." When this remark appeared in *Life* magazine the following April, the negotiations with Kissinger had not even begun, but Mao was already preparing public opinion for the change. Nixon's surprise announcement on July 15 thus came as less of a shock.

Mao did not live to see full normalization of relations; yet he did accomplish a longstanding goal. The Shanghai communiqué, issued at the end of the Nixon visit, recognized that Taiwan was part of China, and that the United States should not intervene in internal Chinese affairs. This meant a giant step forward in resolving the lingering problem of Taiwan. Final resolution of this issue is still in the future.

FINAL DAYS

At the start of the Cultural Revolution, Mao could still appear bronzed and buoyant. Five years later, he could impress Henry Kissinger with his incredible willpower. Then Parkinson's disease began to defeat the man who had bested all his previous opponents. His muscles progressively rigidified and denied him control of his body.

His last public appearance came in August 1973, when he presided over the tenth party congress, called to deal with the problems of reorganization in the wake of the Lin Biao affair. In his final three years, he was confined to his home, where, with great difficulty, he would meet the occasional foreign dignitary or issue terse directives on domestic affairs. Toward the end he lost his capacity to articulate his words; a secretary interpreted his scarcely audible mumbles and poorly scribbled notes.

But his mind remained clear, and he survived, if only by months, many of the original band that had founded the Communist party fifty years earlier. To the dying Zhou Enlai, China's premier and Mao's long-time friend, he dedicated this poem in 1975:

MAO'S EMBALMED BODY IN A CRYSTAL SARCOPHAGUS.

"Loyal parents who sacrificed so much for the
    nation
  Never feared the ultimate fate.
  Now that the country has become Red,
  Who will be its guardians?
  Our mission, unfinished, may take a thousand
    years.
  The struggle tires us, and our hair is gray.
  You and I, old friend, can we watch our efforts
    being washed away?"

Zhou died not long after. Eight months later, on
September 9, 1976, aged 82, Mao Zedong too
finally gave up the struggle.

THE SUCCESSION CRISIS

In his last years, Mao could not overcome the
legacy of the Cultural Revolution's factionalism.
Some of his allies on the left deserted him during
the Lin Biao affair. Revanchists on the right sat in
wait for the inevitable day when he passed from the
scene. A vital center scarcely existed. Until 1976,
the potential conflict was held in check by the
heroic effort of Zhou Enlai, who held the respect of
both camps. After his death, riots followed in the
center of Beijing, but Mao's continued presence
sufficed to force a temporary truce. Mao's passing
removed all restraints. The right staged a successful coup against the left.

Mao may very well have approved of the coup.
He had an impish streak in his historical vision that
allowed nature to take its course. A setback for the
left, in the broadest historical terms, would only
strengthen it by exposing its weaknesses. Certainly
in his final days Mao failed to endorse a leftist-
inspired movement intended to crush the right.
Was this a final rupture with the left which had
already seen several spokespeople castigated as
traitors? Or was it a signal to carry on alone while
their helmsman set his course for a different, distant shore? We will never know.

JIANG QING, MAO'S WIFE, AT THE HEIGHT OF HER POWER IN 1976.

CHINA'S TOP LEADERS JUST BEFORE MAO'S DEATH. TODAY ONLY THE AGING YE JIANYING (SECOND FROM THE RIGHT) AND PREMIER HUA GUOFENG (IN FRONT) ARE STILL IN POWER.

STATUE AT THE ENTRY TO THE MAO MEMORIAL HALL BUILT IN 1977.

POSTSCRIPT: MAO IN CHINA TODAY

There is an ancient Chinese fable called "The Foolish Old Man Who Removed the Mountains." It tells of an old man who lived in northern China long, long ago, and was known as the Foolish Old Man of North Mountain. His house faced south, and beyond his doorway stood two great peaks obstructing the way. With great determination, he led his sons in digging up these mountians, hoe in hand. Another graybeard, known as the Wise Old Man, saw them, and said derisively, "How silly of you to do this! It is quite impossible for you few to dig up these two huge mountains." The Foolish Old Man replied, "When I die, my sons will carry on; when they die, there will be my grandsons, and then their sons and grandsons, and so on to infinity. High as they are, the mountains cannot grow any higher; and with every bit we dig, they will be that much lower. Why can't we clear them away?"

Mao, like the Foolish Old Man in this story, struggled against the two mountains of poverty and oppression weighing down the Chinese people. Unlike the Foolish Old Man, upon whom the gods took pity, sending down angels to remove the mountains, Mao died without reaching his goal. And now China as a nation seems to be putting Mao aside as it marches toward the next century.

But China cannot forget Mao. He made the peaks a little lower and the tasks that much easier for future generations. No matter whether any of his answers were right or wrong, he will always be remembered as the Foolish Old Man who asked of the mountains, "Why can't we clear them away?"

SUGGESTIONS FOR FURTHER READING

Unquestionably the best work on Mao is still Edgar Snow's *Red Star Over China* (New York, 1938, 1961) which contains Mao's autobiography as well as a vivid account of the Chinese communists in 1936.

For a longer, more detailed account of Mao's life, Dick Wilson's *Mao: The People's Emperor* (London, 1979) can be recommended for its liveliness and accuracy. Wilson has also edited a scholarly collection of interpretive essays, *Mao Tse-tung in the Scales of History* (Cambridge, 1977).

Han Suyin, famed for her own multivolume autobiography and numerous novels, completed a two-volume biography of Mao just before his death. The first volume, *The Morning Deluxe* (Boston, 1972), covers up to 1954. *Wind in the Tower* (Boston, 1976) goes to 1975. These volumes are especially strong on the factional struggles in the Chinese Communist party.

One standard scholarly work on Mao is Stuart Schram's *Mao Tse-tung* (Baltimore, 1966). Schram has also edited a number of Mao's writings which have yet to be published officially by the Chinese. Chairman Mao Talks to the People (New York, 1974) is one such work. Another scholarly biography is Jerome Chen's *Mao and the Chinese Revolution* (New York, 1967) which includes 37 poems in translation. Chen also edited *Mao* (Englewood Cliffs, 1969) which adeptly culls quotes from Mao and others to assess Mao and his view of the world.

Many other biographies and works of interpretation exist. The Wilson biography contains an extensive list of them. For those who wish to turn to the history of China itself, a good book with which to start is Maurice Meisner's *Mao's China: A History of the People's Republic* (New York, 1977), which also has an extensive bibliography.

ACKNOWLEDGEMENTS

The author wishes to acknowledge the following for the use of their photos:

René Burri/Magnum, 2-3, 61
Kelly and Walsh, 32, 34-35, 37
UPI, 68, 80, 95, 168, 169
Helen Snow/Magnum, 71
Wide World, 92, 97, 107
Henri Cartier-Bresson/Magnum, 101, 103-104, 108-109, 110, 111
Center for Chinese Studies, 93
Sovfoto, 115, 116

with special thanks going to NCNA and China Pictorial for the remaining photos.